TO: July

Thank you

reading

ded

Jay

Lyn

HEALING MY
FRACTURED
SPIRIT

Glimpses Into My Past

LYNN MILLER

A generous portion of the proceeds from this book will be given,but not limited to the Local and International Charities that we currently support:

The DOVE Center

Dixie Care and Share

New Frontiers for Families

The Covenant House

Food for the Poor

World Vision

Copyright © 2008 by Lynn Miller

All rights reserved. No part of this book may be reproduced in any manner whatsoever without written permission, except in the case of brief quotations embodied in critical articles and reviews.

Printed and bound in Canada

ArtBookbindery.com
Empowering Writers to Self-Publish™

ISBN 978-0-615-23879-1

DEDICATION

This book is dedicated to the hundreds of thousands of hopeless, homeless, orphans, children from broken homes, and those incarcerated, lonely, or depressed.

There is a place for you in society because you are a gift from God and possess unique talents that may be may be in the corner of your soul. Start smiling within yourself and pretty soon it will appear outwardly as you meet and greet other people. *When you smile when no one else is around, you really mean it. – Readers Digest*

Although that precious diamond that has been implanted in you may have been cut, fractured, or crushed, the facets will sparkle even more in the sunlight if you open the door to opportunity. These brilliant hues are the gifts you have been given, and now it is up to you to let their radiance enrich you, but you must try to be less accepted; accepting yourself first. Once you have done this, you have a great start on your way to success.

Never think you are not good enough for anyone; always ask if they are good enough for you.

Anonymous

TABLE OF CONTENTS

ACKNOWLEDGEMENTS

Thank you to my wife Nancy, daughters Laura and Jennifer, son Jeff, son-in-law Jim, daughter-in-law Tami, and grandchildren Kelsi and Landon. Also thanks to the many neighbors and friends who would coax me to relate happenings of my past.

Their initial prodding was for me to write this book after telling tales of my growing up. I was reminded on several occasions of past episodes I related, but had forgotten. Typing, editing, phone calls, and e-mails culminated in the final product – even suggestions for the book title.

My sincere wish is that you enjoy reading "Healing my Fractured Spirit" as much as we all enjoyed arranging the chapters of my life.

INTRODUCTION

This is a story of a boy whose mother died of Tuberculosis when he was three and taken away from his dad along with five other siblings. The all male Parmadale Orphanage where he lived in cottages and attended both school and church would start a firm foundation for his future success. While his father was alive, one sister lived with an uncle and aunt, another with a family outside of Cleveland, Ohio. The youngest sister was adopted at birth only to be found at Ohio State University nineteen years later by her brother, Lynn.

At age six, when his father also died of Tuberculosis, some of the siblings were kept together and others were split up. The foster home, a farm, where Lynn was placed with a brother and sister housed him until he was old enough to leave. It was filled with extreme adversity and hard work. It reeked of mistreatment, malnutrition, and the absconding of his hard earned money for college.

There were many large hurdles through his life, but slowly he walked around them or simply stepped over the smaller ones. It was a long journey, saving again, going to, and graduating from college, and becoming very successful in business.

Today his prayers have been answered for having a loving and caring wife for 47 years as well as children and grandchildren who love him. He prays daily for those less fortunate, and is so thankful that he is able to return some of the gifts given to him as he grew up by donating both time and money to charities and worthy causes.

These stories are moments in time

during my life . . . my story!

INSIDE PARMADALE ORPHANAGE

INSIDE PARMADALE
ORPHANAGE

The secret in life is not what happens to you, but what you do with what happens to you – anonymous

Successful – was something that somehow in the first grade I just knew I was destined to be. It was an absolutely thrilling feeling; my heart was beating so fast. I was smiling from ear to ear, waving to all in the stands as my name was announced for academic as well as athletic achievement. I skipped across the stage with my award, stopped in the center, waved then bowed and skipped off. I thought this is going to go on in my life because I am lucky. I am special and God blessed me and has given me a gift and talent.

Jake - was a handyman at Parmadale and fixed hinges, replaced light bulbs, re-wired radios, repaired lawn mowers and many other jobs that kept him employed at this institution for many years. I met Jake several times; he always had a kind word or smile and was usually whistling while he was working. It seemed everyone loved Jake, and it was very sad when he died unexpectedly of a heart attack. Many of the kids filed by the open casket and I could hear Sister Cecilia saying, "Please don't touch the body" because someone said he is stiffer than a board. Next it was someone rubbing his face exclaiming, "Why did they put so much powder on him because Jake wouldn't have liked that". An older kid, probably in the eighth grade asked Sister why they were burying Jake with his watch on because he wouldn't need it. That did it! In a stern voice Sister said that touching him is a sacrilege and a sin. Most of the kids were not trying to be disrespectful. They just wanted to say good-bye to a friend and to touch him and shake his cold hand. To me even at my young age, he was the father I didn't have and wish I could have had.

The great python escape – at the Cleveland Zoo created quite a stir. I don't know if it was in the newspaper or on the radio, but the word spread rapidly. Upon hearing this, I decided to get a rope from the cottage basement and catch this critter on the loose. On a beautiful and sun-drenched Saturday in late spring I was off to the woods which were directly across the street from Parmadale. I sat quietly on a tree stump waiting for that python to show his face. The sun was warm on my face and before long I was sound asleep. The next thing I knew, something was nudging me on my side. My first thought was the snake was sizing me up. Thank God it was only Sister Anthony asking me what on earth I thought I was doing. When I told her my plan she pointed a finger at me and said, "Listen, that python could swallow you. They get up to 30 feet long and have a mouth bigger than your head." I couldn't get out of the woods fast enough. When I got back to the cottage, Sister sat me down and said she wasn't mad at me; she was just trying to protect me. Then she went on to say how someday I would read in the Bible a story of how Jonah was swallowed by a whale and spit out. I asked if that was because he didn't taste very good. She said, "Well it's a long story, but I saved you from a snake that could have swallowed you into its stomach". I just got goose bumps thinking how dark it would be in there.

Christmas – each year brought a group of men from a local organization who would come to each cottage, line the stairway and sing Christmas carols. Presents were organized by age groups and being in what they call the "baby" cottage, I vividly remember the gifts. Each man took turns calling out a name and handing out a gift. It went like this:

Luke . . . slinky

Josh . . . large plastic spider

Tim . . . huge chocolate bar

Lynn . . . rubber duck

This went on and on until each person had a gift. Of course they were wrapped, but paper would be torn off and the gift announced. It was very nice of these men to visit us and the nuns made sure we thanked them and wished them a Merry Christmas. I tried to swap my rubber duck for the chocolate bar, but Tim said, "No way."

The Pancake Breakfast – came around each spring. It was put on by a local rotary group. You say, "Big deal." Well this was different because they stirred pennies in the batter, cooked them and you could have as many as you wanted as long as you finished one at a time. I never worried about how clean the pennies were because money is money and even today, not many rich people get sick very often, maybe too, because they don't eat pancakes. Some pancakes could have five cents and as many as seven cents. I ate six and collected thirty-six cents which I put in a sock and hid in my drawer.

It's raining golf balls – much to the dismay of one priest at Parmadale who was an avid golfer. This was a sport in which we did not participate. A fellow classmate discovered three large garbage cans full of golf balls and soon the word spread. No doubt these were donated from some local club. The word was out and in short time golf balls were flying. Hundreds, maybe more were bouncing off buildings, rolling down the street and kids were playing catch with them. Father Kimmins was furious when he saw the area snowing with golf balls. He immediately called an assembly in the school auditorium and said he wanted every golf ball put back or there would be punishment for all. We hustled them back in the cans and as we collected our find we were reminded many times on the bull horn that stealing someone else's property was a sin. Most of us felt it wasn't stealing; we just borrowed some golf balls that were given to Father Kimmins.

Busses to Euclid Park – each summer in Sandusky, Ohio, allowed for a day of rides, cotton candy and ice cream. I remember while on the bus looking out at other kids along the way playing in the street, swinging on the porch or just walking like they were bored. I felt sorry for them and wished they could go with us and hoped they weren't jealous. Our bus sign said it all, "Euclid Park for Parmadale

Kids". Each of us had a big square sign around our neck that read, "Parmadale, free food and rides all day".

It was pretty good living at Parmadale . . . and it was going to get even better since I was going to graduate from the "baby" cottage to be with my two older brothers. I woke up one morning outside under a tree, sleeping on just the bed springs. Was I ever scared. After looking around, I was happy to see my oldest brother Jack coming towards me saying over and over, "It's going to be alright, you are moving from the "baby" cottage to the big one with me". My tears disappeared, although I never figured out if this was punishment or if it was something they did to make me feel grown up since I was moving into the big boy's cottage.

FIRSTS

First Confession

I was on a teeter-totter with my friend Josh practicing what we were going to say in that dark closet to a priest. We were really scared and Josh said he would go before me if he could 'borrow' one of my sins I was going to confess. I let him have the one about not obeying four times. He came out of the confessional thumbs up and I felt relieved. I rattled off a, "Bless me Father, for I have sinned." This is my first confession:

1. I lied three times.

2. I did not do homework five times.

3. I think I had a bad thought two times.

4. I got in four fights and won each time.

5. I stole once.

This last one I made up so Josh could have the one about not obeying four times. Father just about floored me when he asked what I stole. I wasn't ready for this! I said, "Well now I remember it was apples." Then he asks, "Did you make restitution?" I did not know what that meant so I said, "No, I just ate them," and I could hear Father laugh so I left the confessional. Later I told Josh and he said he thought restitution was some kind of recipe. We compared punishment for our sins; Josh got six Hail Mary's. I got almost the same but Father added a Glory Be and Our Father.

First Communion

Sister Cecilia told me to go to the barbershop and get my haircut before the big day Sunday. She said she wanted my appearance to go with the white shorts, socks, shirt and tie so I looked pure to the visiting Bishop. On the way to the barber, Tony, a second grader, asked me to play baseball because they were one person short. I said I couldn't because I needed to get a haircut for my first communion tomorrow. He said he would cut it for me when the other players were resting. He went on to say he had scissors and a ruler to part my hair, but no mirror. He said with the sun behind me I could see my shadow against the building and assured me he would do a good job. When I returned after baseball, with my hair cut, the nuns didn't know if they should laugh or cry. I looked in the mirror and wow, what a chopping Tony did. The next morning when I looked up at the Bishop, he chuckled out loud and had a glimmer in his eye. Oh Lord, please forgive Tony he was just trying his best. Besides, he needed an extra player.

FIRST FOSTER HOME

One day our social worker brought my brother Mike and me to the foster home, a farm, where we would be living, to introduce us to three Daly women. Anna, to be our foster mother, was about 56 years old and her daughters Loretta, age 32, and Jane, age 28. There was no man as the husband or father. He had been trampled by a team of horses when a swarm of bees attacked them and threw him off the equipment. I learned later that we were just a few of the many who were dropped off for periods of time ranging from a few months to a year. Unfortunately, we were to live with them for eleven years. Our sister, Dorothy, who was living with a family in Elyria, was also brought to this farm. The very first night we were there, I got a spanking for grabbing bunches of cherries off a tree in the backyard, carrying them upstairs and eating them. The eating part wasn't so bad but I sat in the upstairs window and spit the cherry pits outside through the open window. They landed on the steps to the basement and Loretta slid on them and came rushing up to our bedroom with a stick that she swatted me with. This would be the first of many spankings, whippings, beltings, and slaps that I received. A week later my brother and I got into a pillow fight. Imagine a chicken coop with 40 chickens fighting in an 8x10 room. Feathers were flying all over the place and soon the door flew open and in comes Loretta saying, "Okay smart alecks, you will pick up every feather and put them back in the cases since you won't be needing them anymore." Oh well, I thought they gave me a stiff neck anyway, I reasoned to myself. As the early months and years passed so did the many times I got in trouble. The stress of each day took its toll even though I did my best to be positive. It was very frustrating when I often got punished for so many things including smiling, laughing, or singing. I walked in my sleep, wet the bed, talked in my sleep, and ground my teeth. More than once I would be awakened by my brother, sister, or one of the Daly's telling me to stop grinding my teeth.

One day while walking through the strawberry patch I noticed a one pound coffee can containing four baby kittens. Pretty soon, while I watched, this wild mother cat came hissing at me and took them one by one in her mouth, climbing up a tree, moving them to safe place. I wanted to continue to watch so I got a ladder and climbed up to see the kittens. I was getting close when a swarm of bees attacked my hands. Immediately the tops of my hands swelled as though I was wearing boxing gloves. I had been stung by at least forty bees. Over time the swelling went down, but it still hurt. There were many remedies in my foster house for whatever ailed you. One day, as I was feeding the cows, I reached into a feed box and a rat bit me on the finger. This time it was just my one finger that swelled but every day for several days Loretta and Jane would hold my hand in boiling water to get rid of the infection. This hurt very much and I remember screaming loudly. Thankfully, a nurse who worked at the General Industries plant with Loretta and Jane called and said she needed a ride because her car wouldn't start. She was told of my finger and came by, got a needle, sterilized it with a match, and punctured my swollen finger. The fluid from inside shot up to the ceiling, I felt so much relief. Thankfully . . . no more boiling water for my finger. The neighbor nurse said to Ma Daly, "I thought you said you were a practical nurse." She replied, "No, I said I was practically a nurse." The real nurse applied some salve she had in her purse and put on a band-aid. It wasn't long before my finger was back to normal.

Other solutions for medicinal use would be Cod-liver oil every day for the first week in March to flush you out. It tasted awful, but we were told it was for "spring cleaning". Two or three bulbs of garlic on a string around your neck was a certain cure for sore throat and bag balm applied to the cows utter in summer was great for a sun burn or to prevent one. Acne was solved with a good brushing with Fels Naphtha or Lava, leaving your face beet red. Starve a cold or feed a fever, at our house it was used interchangeably. During the many times I had pneumonia the only solid or liquid was hot tea.

A cold was a cold and never hampered doing chores, working, or going to school.

In my eleven years in the foster home I was never hugged, kissed, or had a good night or good morning salutation. The A's and B's in school meant nothing, but all P's for poor conduct was the thing they looked at and commented on. I wanted and needed attention and would tell jokes in class and imitated Amos and Andy who I heard on the radio. Most conversations were negative, even getting a slap or a belt whipping for laughing or smiling. I would hear, "Why do you sing or laugh or smile? What's so great that you are always happy like you got something over on us." I remember the words said so many times by Loretta and Jane, "You don't do that here, maybe when you get older." I always thought, older than what? My brother Mike and sister Dolly (Dorothy) would tell me over and over to keep my mouth shut rather than argue. That is why I got so many punishments. When I would hear, "You are not going to amount to nothing," I would fire back, "Oh yes I am!" I figured by arguing at least I was not aiding and abetting the enemy. Saying nothing was like telling them I agreed.

Who can protest and does not, is an accomplice in the act
—The Talmud

On the day of your birthday your soul lights a candle to celebrate being born and alive that special day. Now I thought that candle was lit sometime in the fall each year because that's when my oldest sister Marlene told me I was born. Up until the time I asked her that question, thirteen uncertain years had gone by. I knew I was getting closer to the exact date when she said my cousin Larry and I were born in November sometime. It never was a big thing at the foster home because no one really celebrated anyone's birthday. No cakes, ice cream, presents, toys, or parties. I read that back through history the only documented birthdays were of kings and other noble dignitaries. The poorer people, especially children, did not celebrate at all. It is the German's who have been given credit for starting to celebrate children's birthdays. These celebrations were called Rinder feste, meaning children's festival. Maybe the Daly's thought was, "Why celebrate a German tradition?" when they were Irish through and through.

As I got older the punishments grew harsher. More often than not I was singled out for my happy go lucky attitude, singing, or smiling. At first it was a slap in the face, then a whipping with a willow branch, later came the 2"x4" or a lashing with a belt, all of them inflicted by any of the three Daly women. Sometimes I thought having to go to bed without dinner, especially with the meager meals before, was worse than the physical abuse. One cold fall Friday evening, I had just come into the basement after hauling wood on a sled from the side of the barn. My hands were cold and my teeth were chattering. I stood in front of the furnace rubbing my hands and face when out of the darkness appeared Loretta, whom I thought of as "the beast". She had now graduated to a new weapon to inflict maximum pain, the iron poker used to shake ashes from the bottom of the furnace. As I was leaning toward the furnace, I felt a blow across the shoulders that almost knocked me over. She continued and I could hear her grunt between thrusts and my screaming. Jane came bolting down the stairs and shoved Loretta against the wall. "What in the hell do you think you are doing? You could cripple him for life!" Maybe that was her intent. I learned later she had done the same thing to my sister who still has the scars.

FEED SACK SHIRTS

In hard times feed sacks made pretty good shirts for me and blouses for Loretta and Jane. Once in a while they would make me a dress white shirt from a flour bag. Usually they would go to the General Feed Store in Oberlin to pick out feed and their favorite patterns which were mostly flowered, but sometimes just mixed colors. This reminded me of Dolly Parton when she expressed in her song, My Coat of Many Colors that my Mama Made for Me. Mike opted for the hand me downs from people in the city and said to Jane and Loretta that I liked the home made shirts the best, so I got them. It wouldn't have been so bad, but the pattern they used was for Loretta about a 38C and Jane a 38D which didn't quite hang or adjust right on my thin frame. They cut the pattern down a bit, but at 5'3" and 87 pounds, it was just a funny fit. The first button was between my neck and navel and the sleeves were like long balloons narrowing down to a cuff. The lapels were quite large and thankfully I didn't live in tornado alley or on one of those blustery days, I could have flown home.

Good Things Come in Small Packages

We had a Christmas gift exchange in the third grade and the nuns had the boy's names in one box and the girls in the other. They would draw a name from each and alphabetically give out the slip with a name. My slip had the name of Diane, who later was my girlfriend in the eighth grade. I was so excited coming home, saying I needed a present for a girl in a gift exchange in our class. I did not see what Loretta wrapped but it looked nice and even had a bow. When Diane opened the package from Lynn Miller, we both gasped. It was a bar of Fels Naphtha Soap.

Time heals all wounds, love speeds up the process
— Nina Terol

THE POWER OF PRAYER

THE POWER OF PRAYER

High hopes give you a chance to be disappointed
–Adrian Moonshine

Prayer to me is like talking to God and if you would just stop and listen for awhile, He will talk to you. I talk to God often, not as much asking for favors, but seeking answers and expecting only what He planned for me. I always knew I wanted Him and needed Him as a Friend in solitude. This belief has always been a part of my life since I was in kindergarten and continues today. I mentioned in chapter one how great I felt accepting the two awards in first grade. I thanked my Friend and said not to worry; I would pay Him back and make Him proud. At the foster home I prayed every night on my knees and even said a prayer to St. Michael (my brother's name) the Arch Angel so someday he would join me on the floor. He never did.

In the fifth grade the nuns repeatedly told us about the power of prayer and God would give us an answer or a sign if we prayed hard enough. This seemed at first to be a very young age to be telling about the power of prayer, but it wasn't for material things, health or good grades. It was for a vocation. We were to pray and listen to God for His reply whether we should marry, remain single, or dedicate our lives to becoming a priest or nun. I took this very seriously and looked in my sock drawer so I would know exactly where I planned to tell God to put His answer to my important question. That night I said a special prayer, "Dear God, if you want me to be a priest, put a small note, even a yes or no will do, in my black and yellow argyle socks in the top drawer. I have pushed all the other socks aside so these will sit by themselves in the right hand corner. I usually get up around 6:00am to do chores but if you need more time I will make a second check before going to school at 7:30am." Usually I fall asleep right away, but this was a special night. What if God put a note in my socks, either a yes or no would even be a holy and wonderful sign. Blessed Mary appeared in Fatima, Portugal to Lucia, Francisco and Jacinta, and they were just poor children, but look at the shrine that was built in her honor. I met the criteria for the poor and there were 40 acres where plenty of cars could park if the sign appears. I imagined crutches, wheel chairs, canes, and people with sicknesses coming from around the world to be cured. Thank you God, this could be the spot because we had plenty of water in the well and creek if people wanted to bring home holy water. There could be a sign on our road that read, "Shrine ahead, 3 miles on the right." The next morning I woke up at 5:00am and did not want to look in the socks too early so I waited another hour. I didn't tell a soul and wanted my bedmates Ma Daly and Mike to get up before I opened the drawer. I finally checked and carefully unfolded the socks because if God had touched them they would be very holy . . . nothing. No note was found even when I made the second check before going to school. I told God that night I understood; I would probably get married and not feel badly. At recess I told my friend Chet of my deal with God and to keep it secret because laughing about this was not in His favor. What a blessing telling Chet in confidence, he told me his parents went to Italy or Egypt a few years ago and the time difference was seven or eight hours. We went back right away to the classroom to get some paper and pencil and figured out roughly the distance to God's home in heaven had to be four or five times further than to either country his parents went to. We agreed with a secret hand shake that I would wait another week to give God time to think it over because a holy person, Chet said, doesn't like to be rushed. The special socks were never even touched, but slowly opened after the given time and showed nothing. I felt better for not rushing His decision and I was happy all over.

Even before the tornado struck and littered the yard and cow pasture with debris, things on the Daly Ranch for wayward children weren't going so well. Several things happened and I must admit most were my innocent doing. Once I was asked to fill the tractor with gas and did not shut off the engine when I pulled it next to the large gas drum. It caught on fire and burned the motor and most of the paint around it. Soon after Jane purchased a new red Buick convertible with an Isinglass (sort of tough plastic) back window you could zip open. She kept her "pride and joy" in the barn and one day I pitched a bale of hay from the loft and it landed perfectly inside it, like right through the Isinglass. Several months later the dilapidated granary next to the corn crib was set on fire and we were all positioned with bats and brooms to kill the scores of rats that called it home. The Daly's had purchased a rat terrier puppy with great blood lines for $75. He was prancing around and we were told not to rely on him to catch a rat because he was too young and just learning the trade. As the fire got more intense, the rats started to come out. Everybody was swinging and with one fell swoop I killed the biggest rat and the terrier chasing it. Luckily I wasn't punished because it was just bad timing. It was this same evening they decided we should all say the family Rosary with Father Patrick on the radio every night at 6:30pm. The reception on our radio was poor and sporadic with lots of static. If you're tuning was just right the voice was a little clearer. We were to say the rosary every night for three weeks because it was a Novena like for special requests. I never knew what the special requests were but I am sure Daly's were thinking no more bad luck and keep Lynn away from things that could get broken. About the fourth day Loretta and Jane were taking turns trying to tune in Father Patrick and the rosary. They were seated in the front now with the radio between them and the rest of us were on our knees in the back of the room with one exception, I had my leg in a cast so I got to sit. Occasionally I would lower my voice and say Hail Mary full, then stop and from all evil Amen and stop. Loretta and Jane were swatting each other because each thought they had the right reception. I should have stopped when I was ahead, but was having too much fun. Mike and Dolly were cracking up and just as I let out another, Our Father who and trailed off, Loretta turned around. I was caught red handed. They were both embarrassed for falling for my prank and I was going to pay for it. Loretta stood up, shook her fist at me and said, "Okay smart ass, you are going to lead the rosary for the remainder of the Novena," which was almost two and a half weeks. She was really mad! Can you even imagine swearing right before saying the Holy rosary? I think God was trying to tell the Daly's that they had it all wrong. Perhaps that is why the radio reception was so poor. My thinking is you don't pray after the storm, but before and if you got the storm anyway and it was bad, be thankful it wasn't worse. When one of us wouldn't admit to breaking something or doing wrong, we were asked to go to communion Sunday and since it was a mortal sin they said to lie, the one that didn't go was guilty. Usually I would fess up since most of the time I was at the heart of the problem and didn't want to lie.

Lent was a special time for prayers. We had separate "stations" to pray on our knees for a half hour each day and three hours on Good Friday. I chose the corn crib and although it was tough on the knees, I had visions of gold in the kernels. The Farm Bureau offered $25,000 to anyone finding an ear with an odd number of rows. I must have counted a thousand ears of corn and it was only after I took a genetics course in college did I learn it was impossible to have an odd number of rows on a cob! I didn't feel badly though because now I knew no one else beat me counting to win the prize. I didn't know all the stations we were assigned to pray, but I do recall Dolly being on the gravel pathway that led to the well and pump. Carmen and Maria were in the second and third grade and had cut a hole in a burlap bag and slid it over their heads and were kneeling on the steps of the front porch. Talk about doing penance in sack cloth! It was amazing how often those hypocrites, the Daly's, would rely on prayer, medals, statues, and even holy water. We even had a statue of the Blessed Virgin Mary in the upstairs hallway and during May we would cut violets from the woods and put them in a vase before her.

A hypocrite carries his Bible under his arm, but not in his heart. His whole religion is a demure lie – Thomas Watson

The eve of confirmation all those to be confirmed were to meet in the church basement thirty minutes or so before the service for final instructions. As I walked across the parking lot I was wondering how I looked in comparison with the other kids. My wool suit, even with the cuffs let out, was still too short and tight. My homemade white shirt from a flour sack, the oil stain on my right knee and this big red ribbon for a tie probably was unique. As I peeked in the basement window all of my wondering came to real life. All the boys had neat store bought white shirts, nice suits, but more than anything else, each one had a red neck tie. The red tie was a mandatory thing to signify your wish and right to defend the church's teachings. There was not a word or even a snicker as I came into the room and sat down for the instructions. I had no idea who my sponsor was as most kids met theirs earlier and it would be a relative or someone in back of the church that walked them down the aisle. I just went and sat down when this big man with a gruff voice came into the pew, sat down and asked me if I was the Miller kid. When I said yes, he handed me an envelope that I opened right away and I was smiling from ear to ear when I saw a new $5 bill. All the church music was blocked out of my mind as I was thinking of what to do with the money. At first squirt guns came to me, but the latest fads were yo-yo's and that was that. Ben Bitner the local undertaker was my sponsor and when it was our turn he walked down the aisle with me. I took Nicholas for my confirmation name because to me it had a double meaning. Nick was a tough short version of Nicholas and although I didn't want to project that, it sounded good. St. Nicholas' feast day, December sixth, is kept alive and honored through the stories of his goodness and generosity. He is so loved and revered as a protector and helper of those in need. So you see I chose a perfect name. On the way back from the altar where the Bishop confirmed you, I was looking up to the choir loft to see who was singing so pretty. I didn't realize until I sat down that my red ribbon tie had fallen off. In the back of the church a lady handed me my tie and said I looked so handsome and I reminded her of Little Lord Fauntleroy. Several years later at the library I looked up Little Lord Fauntleroy and found out Frances Hodgson Burnett wrote a famous story of a New York street urchin who finds out he is the heir to a fortune and a British title. I guess I didn't look so bad after all. I never did get to be an heir and the only title I ever had was Director of World Wide Sales towards the end of my business career. Saturday morning I woke up early and reached under the sheet by my head to make sure the $5 was still there. After chores and breakfast I asked permission to go to the library in town while my real purpose was to buy a few yo-yo's. The clerk at the store said the best value was to buy the unpainted ones and get some glass chips and other pieces to decorate them. I got a ride home with one of the neighbors who just happened to be in town shopping. I ran up our hill and found my brother Mike doing something in the barn. When I told him of my purchase he suggested we paint them right from the can of paint used to touch up the Farmall tractor. I thought I better tell Jane and Loretta what I used some of the money for and gave them the $2.90 in change. Now I am off to the granary with Mike who suggested I open the can of paint, place it on a stool and just lower each yo-yo then hang them up to dry and we could decorate them later. This paint job was easy, but just as I got them all done and hung up, I backed into the can and spilled paint all over the place. Thank goodness we had been given a bag of shirts and pants from somebody because I needed another set. It wasn't important about size or color; pants were pants and shirts were shirts. Mike said he would go to the house and get me a change of clothes. We cleaned up and took the painted clothes to an old abandoned well in the barnyard. About two years later we had an abundance of rain and Ma Daly said she thought we could clean the old well for storing water that was running in. We lowered these hay bale hooks because she thought she saw some clothing at the bottom of the well. When we brought up the shirt and pants, she said they must have belonged to her late husband. You could tell they had been here for awhile because they had shrunk. I felt so relieved and never said a word. Although Ma Daly was probably in her early sixties, she was getting very forgetful. Often she would get our names mixed up calling me Mike, Roger, Clarence, and then finally blurting out the right name. I never said a word or thought differently, after all there was a herd of kids at one time or another staying at the Daly Ranch and it could get very confusing. At her funeral, years later, I learned that 43 children had passed through her home. Of the 43, I was the only one who attended her services.

IF NECESSITY IS THE MOTHER OF INVENTION, I WAS HER MOST INNOVATIVE STEP-CHILD

IF NECESSITY IS THE MOTHER OF INVENTION, I WAS HER MOST INNOVATIVE STEP-CHILD

Everything you can imagine is real
- Pablo Picasso

Some of my favorite things:

1. Two of the popular chewing gums most of the kids had at school were Cinnamon and Black Jack, both made by Beemans. I didn't think we had cinnamon around, but our county road had plenty of tar and with a little sugar you had a decent chew. The secret was to get the tar in the morning when it could easily be rolled and sliced through to check for pebbles. I had many happy chews and it was free.

2. There was a basketball hoop that must have been donated and Jane fastened it to the side of the barn. I would guess it would have been about 12 feet high and did not have a net. We found the shell of a basketball at the dump and stuffed it with rags. Although it made playing a little awkward, it was good practice for intramural games or the occasional pick-up game on Saturday. A good thing was not having to chase the ball after it came down since it didn't bounce. No wonder I held the individual high game and average scoring record for several years in the 7th and 8th grade.

3. People would leave or bring over boxes or bags of clothes, games, or books. It reminded me of leftovers from a garage sale. In one large full bag there were twenty checkers, ten red

and ten black and I looked frantically, but no checker board. Not finding one I chose the next best thing, the kitchen floor. It was black and white checked and made it difficult to play checkers so we played a different game. We lined up each color across from each other and took turns shooting across the floor with the goal of knocking your opponent's checkers out of its square. The one with the most checkers on the squares after a given time was the winner. I vividly remember the first game I played with my sister Dolly. Loretta was downstairs doing laundry and when she was almost to the top of the stairs shouted, "What on earth is that racket?" After that we never played when she was downstairs. We knew better than to push our luck.

4. Some of the nuns must have noticed I didn't wear socks May through October. There was no way they could have known no underwear was worn during these months either. One day a big bag of matched socks was delivered to our house and now there were socks galore. Jane or Ma Daly got this brain storm that by just sewing the sides of the heels for your thumb, you could have a cheap pair of colorful gloves. Brother Mike said he rarely got cold hands, but knew I said many times that I wish I had gloves. Oh well, all the other boys had boring black or brown gloves while mine were red and black, black and gold, green and black, and even orange and brown. I thought how cool I was wearing matching socks and gloves. It was no wonder I never heard anyone ask, like they do at the Academy Awards ceremonies, "Who dressed you today?"

5. The rope tied through a tire then wrapped around a sturdy tree limb made a great swing, but this was, and maybe still is quite common in the country. Finding the right grapevine secured to a tree and long enough to bring you out over the river so you could let go in the middle was a different feat. I found three of these along the Black River, but didn't really consider these innovations, just good discoveries.

6. When I fished in the city park for the biggest fish and won, all of the city kids had Shakespeare or Zebco reels on nice eyelet rods. I knew from past experience that fish are not fussy as to

what gear you are using. Up until a month or so ago I had a branch with kite string, a good hook for a fat worm and it worked. One day at school, I noticed a broken, hand-cranked pencil sharpener in the waste basket and asked Sister Mary Rose if I could have it. She nodded yes and the expression on her face said, "I wonder what on earth he's going to do with that?" Opportunity sat there at the bottom of the waste basket and I took it. I was so excited I hitch-hiked home to beat the bus, did my chores in a hurry and headed for the barn with my find. At first I tried to fasten the pencil sharpener to the pole with screws, but stopped when the wood started to crack. I found some electrical tape that once was put over my mouth for sassing back and fastened the reel to the pole. It worked! I got my kite filament line and threaded it through some screw eyelets I placed up the pole and I now had first class fishing gear. This sturdy put together lasted for years, helped me catch many fish and was my pride and joy because I made it.

7. For most, Halloween was a fun evening going around the neighborhood, but walking several miles round trip to visit only nine or ten houses was a challenge in patience. The neighbors all knew us and some of them just to be kind would say things like, "I have no idea who this could be." My costume was creative to say the least. I wore Jane's trench coat and carried a sign that had a gun drawn on the top and bottom that read Detective. Another year I wore the same trench coat, carried Loretta's camera and had a card taped to each side of my hat that read 'The Press'. Lots of candy and secret dollar bills made the effort worth it.

8. It seemed that most of the kids at school with money from lucrative allowances had the newest toys or fads on the market. We went through the stages of code rings, bubble gum cards, yo-yo's, squirt guns, and the newest, walkie-talkies. Not having the money to buy one, I saved a couple of soup cans, had plenty of string, now my own walkie-talkie was born. I carefully pounded a hole in the center of each can, inserted the string tied a large knot to secure it and had a beauty with 30 feet of cord. I asked Mike to try out my innovation with me and at

first it wasn't very good, but it seemed to work a little. While doing chores I got a brilliant idea, maybe it would help rubbing the cord with soap to keep the fibers from letting the sound out and keeping it along the line. Upon trying this I got so excited since it seemed to work, especially when I used a louder voice. My imagination helped me to have things that I otherwise wouldn't have. It got me through many lonely times.

Near the End of the Rainbow I Found . . . Mushrooms

Sunday it rained all day with just a slight drizzle that soaked the ground. After church and a heaping dish of pancakes everyone but me was headed for the usual Sunday snooze. On the way home we saw a beautiful rainbow that was very intense in color and I decided to explore while they were napping. In case anyone asked I already planned to say I was going to the river to catch some minnows for fishing. My real goal was to find out for myself what was at the end of the rainbow. Was it a pot of gold or was it maybe diamonds? I decided which ever one was found, would be shared with the whole family. Walking though the field it was apparent I wasn't getting any closer to the end of the rainbow. What I did find was just as special and unique and caused me to stop and gaze. At first I thought I was seeing masses of white flames in clusters, but the closer I got I realized they were clumps of mushrooms. Taking out my jackknife I cut at the base of each mushroom and I couldn't cut fast enough because there were so many. Soon the five gallon pail was full and it took all my strength to carry it a little distance, but I would rest then head home. When I got home it was around four P.M. and back at the Daly house most were shaking the cob webs out of their heads. I ran to show a handful of my find to Jane and she asked, "How would we know if they are poisonous?" I suggested she call Frank the local extension agent and see if he could come by; or could we bring him a sample to evaluate? He said he was invited to dinner a few houses from us and would stop by on the way. He took one look and said they are rare and special because they are morels. You could tell he said by the honeycomb texture and cone shape and went on to say they were more sought after than regular mushrooms for their unique flavor. He estimated the value around seventy-five cents a quart so my five gallon pail had twenty quarts that could fetch $15. Jane got on the phone to co. workers and after several calls all were sold. The county agent said mushrooms grew overnight and the harvest period was very short. With that in mind I stayed home Monday and Tuesday and gathered three more pails that I left in the field for Jane or Mike to pick up later. Like the first batch, these sold quickly and my new find saw another source of income besides picking fruit, berries, beans, cutting grass, and baby-sitting. Jane said she would reward me by putting money in a Christmas club. I forgot about this and so did Jane. I made the household happy for a few days.

The best way to cheer yourself up is to cheer everybody else up
– Mark Twain

FAKE ID

It was my last year in grade school and we were asked to bring our baby picture. The pictures would be pinned on the wall with a cardboard cup beneath each one. Everyone had to write on a slip of paper who they thought the baby was and put it in the cup. You could guess as many times as you wanted, except not for yourself, and with each guess you had to put in a dime. After three days the votes were tallied and the winner was allowed to send the money to a charity in India in his or her name. The winner was the child with the most incorrect guesses in their cup. I won hands down, but I cheated slightly! Since I did not have a baby picture, I borrowed one from a neighbor who had only two girls. Luckily one had light brown hair. The faded picture showed this little three year old girl standing next to a horse. It worked well that she was wearing a cowboy hat to cover up her curly hair. This is the first time I have told this story. Bless me Father, for I lied once!

SNAKES AND SNAILS AND PUPPY DOG TAILS

It is said that's what little boys are made of. I didn't mind the snails and puppy dog tails, but I didn't want any part of a snake. I mentioned in an earlier chapter my escapade hunting down the python that escaped from the zoo…now to me that wasn't scary. I did have two more encounters that sent shivers down my spine. One hot dry summer day, when I was ten years old and headed to the creek to fish when I spotted an all black colored snake about one and a half feet long lying on a rock soaking up some sun. I decided to pet him and as I got closer it jumped up at me, and I fell backwards, got up and then ran home. When I told Jane, she said that was a water moccasin and they were poisonous. Thoughts of having my hand boiled ran through my mind and I shook all over. The following spring we had the usual floods that prompted my poems, and I was watching a pile of brush slowly floating down the creek. My eyes grew wider when I thought what I saw was a new bike tire with deep treads. Fetching a long stick I pulled the brush over and reaching for the tire I saw a pair of eyes. After tossing the stick to the side, my legs couldn't get me home fast enough. I found out later from a neighbor that was a black snake and they grow large, but are harmless.

Who could forget the story from Sister Rose Ann. She would read us a letter from missionaries in India and afterwards a little box was passed around where we put change in for the poor. The letter read how the missionaries were exposed to Cobra's because they were so common. They always had to be on guard especially at dawn and dusk. After reading the letter sister went on to say how the cobra should remind us of the devil. He tempts us just like the face of the cobra with things that, at the time, look awesome and mesmerizing. When we fall to temptations or agree to do bad things, the cobra bites you from the other end, the end that most think is the tail. I am so glad I learned later she had it all backwards. They say snakes can smell fear, perhaps the odor our bodies give off, this too makes me think of the devil finding our weaknesses.

If your eyes are blinded with your worries,
you cannot see the beauty of the sunset or animals
- Krishnamurti

VETERINARIAN OR SALES?

Through my efforts I placed three girls and three boys in foster homes; farm homes in the neighborhood. Jane gathered up six kittens for me from two litters, put them in a burlap bag and told me to take them to the creek. She said by the edge of the water there should be some stones to be added to the bag. I was then instructed to throw everything into the deep part of the creek. I asked, and was given permission to take the cuties around the neighborhood and find them a good home. I had to practice my sales pitch and rest because it was hot and the three mile round trip would be tiring. I named each kitten and had the same sales pitch for each. Carrying the bag of fur in my arms, I stopped at the creek and watered the bag down to keep my friends cool. At my first stop I lifted out Clancy and said I really believe you are going to like him because his daddy was a real mouser; sneaked up on them quietly and pounced. Never ever did he miss! Now Clancy has bright eyes because he's alert and by his purr you can tell he likes you. Of course there is no fee, the only thing I ask is that you be good to your new friend. I promised to stop by once in awhile just to see how things are going. Then I left, thanking them from the bottom of my heart. One down, five to go! My sales pitch worked and I felt confident placing the others would not be difficult. With Clifton and Chad I used the same words I did with Clancy. The only change I made with Chelsea, Cecilia, and Charlotte was their mother was a real mouser. Of course, I added the part about the bright eyes and the purr. Luckily I placed all six kittens and one farm family even gave me a dollar which I hid in a band-aid can in the basement. I ran part way home with the empty bag, thinking to myself, if I don't become a vet, I will sell stuff. As I got closer to the creek, I peeled off my shirt, took off my shoes and jumped in to cool down and to celebrate my rescue.

We can judge the heart of a man by his treatment of animals
- Immanuel Kant

My Frozen Footed Feathered Friend

Up until the seventh grade, holiday breaks at Christmas and Easter were fun times because we could stay up until eight rather than be in bed by 7:30. In later years, I used these breaks to work and earn money. One Saturday evening, the week before Christmas, I was feeling house bound and was eager to get out and build a snow fort or go ice skating . After dinner everyone else elected to stay in where it was warm and watch television. I asked if I could go ice-skating with the promise to be back before 8pm, it was now 6:30. The ice skates I had were hand-me-downs from somebody and were a size ten. I must have been about a size seven because it took two small potatoes in the toe to help them fit somewhat properly. It was in the high 30's during the day, but at night with the temperature dropping, it probably dropped to the mid 20's. This clear night was cold and quiet with the moon shining on the creek. As I was sitting on the shore to put on my skates, I noticed a dark figure on the ice. At first, I thought it was a small dog. On further inspection I saw it was a mallard duck that may be injured or even dead. As I slowly approached the duck he tried to move, but couldn't, because his feet were frozen to the ice. I named the duck Chuck and told him I would be back to help him. From the barn I got a bushel basket, the sled, an axe, and stopped by the granary to get a couple ears of corn. I flew back down the hill to help my new friend Chuck. I slowly got to the duck out on the ice and chopped carefully around his legs, lifting he and the ice block into the bushel basket and then onto the sled. I shucked some corn so Chuck could have something to eat on the way home. It was quite a pull but I got my friend safely up the hill to the basement stairs and carried him in. I placed Chuck by the furnace so he could get warm and thaw his feet. After shelling some more corn I got a small pan of water and placed it on the floor. I left a light on over the "zink" so he wouldn't be afraid during the night and went upstairs. I never did get to ice-skate, but I did a good deed that made me feel good all over. When I told the Daly's of my episode they said okay, but the duck should go in the morning. I woke up a little early, dressed and scurried to the basement. My new friend met me at the bottom of the stairs with a quack, quack, quack. I tucked him under my arm and took him back to the creek to join his other friends who were sleeping on the bank with their heads under their wings to keep warm.

Animals share with us the privilege of having a soul
- Pythagoras

NEIGHBORLY ADVICE

Ben Carter was a nice neighbor and the only African-American with a wife and several kids in the whole county. He had this wonderful tree that had apples the size of grapefruit. One time I got a stick and was swatting some apples over the fence and out came Ben. He taught me a great lesson . . . "Just ask me next time and you are always welcome, but just don't sneak over, that is not a good neighbor." I thanked him, shook his hand and said he was a nice man. Several weeks later when I was swatting another apple, this time with his permission, he said to be careful of the Black River behind our house. When he had been cat-fishing there he discovered a huge snapping turtle on a large flat rock. Enough said, I ran home to get a wheel-barrow, rope, shovel and bag. It took some doing, but I got the snapper and wheeled him home so he could later be sold by Jane to a restaurant for seventy cents per pound or $12.75 for the seventeen pounder. What I did at every chance to earn money for "the cause", not mine.

A Manure Pile and the Birds and Bees

One of only two movies, both Irish, which I had seen in eleven years was <u>Fighting O' Flynn</u>, the other was <u>My Wild Irish Rose</u>. I was impressed with the former picture. I don't remember much of the movie, but I do know he was a good guy for rescuing a dame in need. Coming home I was envisioning the pole vault and what I would use as a barrier to sail over. The next day was Sunday and as soon as everyone at my house crashed, after a heavy noon meal, I decided to try my luck at vaulting. By the clothesline was a hickory pole about eight feet long that was used to prop up wet clothes on the sagging line. The only mound that would be safe if I missed was the manure pile behind the barn. Just in case I missed I had changed into my swimming suit. I practiced running and planting the pole four or five times until I was confident I could make it. Now I was ready. I made the sign of the cross, ran even further than in practice, planted the pole and landed three-quarters of the way up the ten foot pile of manure. I could hear the pigs snorting; their way of laughing I guess. I climbed carefully down the pile shook myself off and headed for the creek across the road. There was a nice flow of water in the creek and I found a nice waterfall. At first I lay on my back and splashed water all around, then got a bar of lava soap that I had stored nearby under a bush for emergencies like this. I soaped up and checked thoroughly to see if anyone was watching or coming. I slipped off my swim trunks and with my chin on the rocks beneath the falls let the water "wrench" me off. Since my maiden jump hadn't taken very long and everyone was in snore heaven back at the house, I just lay there listening to the birds, watching butterflies as they floated by and watching bumble bees busy on the clover blossoms. I needed to dry off so I headed back to the barnyard and since it was a hot eight-five degrees, I decided to climb up on the roof of the pig pen and let the sun dry both me and my swim suit. With my head hanging over the edge of the roof all five piglets were looking up at me. There was Violet, Daisy, Blossom, Petunia, and their boy friend Oscar. Looking at their faces reminded me of a saying from General George S. Patton Jr., he said "I like pigs, dogs look up to us, cats look down on us, but pigs treat us as equals." I told them my story and the little piglets seemed to understand. Suddenly I was asleep, when I woke up I was dry. I scrambled down from the roof, cleaned and replaced the pole, changed back into my clothes, and got a book to read until the rest got up from their naps. What a day I had experienced. After finishing a couple of chapters of <u>The Biography of Nathan Hale</u>, I marked the page where I had left off, closed my eyes and said "Thank you God, this has been a great day." There had been plenty of sun, a flowing stream, fish, fresh air, butterflies, bees, frogs, blue sky, and it was so quiet. During my adventurous day I never saw another person or even a car passing along. I smiled to myself and thought of this day that everyone else had missed. Just think, if I had made it past the manure pile, I could have missed all of those. Knowing myself, if I had cleared the pile on my first vault, I would have tried more and more to establish a personal record and ended up in the creek anyway.

I have never the companion that was so companionable as solitude
- Henry David Thoreau

SOME LIGHTER MOMENTS

Some Lighter Moments

The future belongs to those who believe in the beauty of their dreams
— Eleanor Roosevelt

I was always quite adventurous and discussed with Mike the idea of walking to the Black River behind our house. He said to go ahead and let him know what I find. My hope was to find some muskrat traps that may have been lost, washed aground, or just left behind from the past trapping season. My eyes bulged in misbelief when I found, of all things in the reeds, a boat. Although it was far from complete, it had sides, one board on the back and no bottom. Talk about a find, just think . . . I found a boat! Although it was missing some parts, it had what I thought was a key item, the sides. How on earth does one bend boards and curve them like that? The quarter mile run home seemed to take forever and I told Mike of my find. We could even let neighbor Rudy in as a partner because his brother worked at the Farm Bureau and maybe he could get us some used lumber for free. We spent several evenings in the corner of the barn preparing a spot and hauling in nails, tar paper, shingles, boards, and whatever we could think of to build our boat. Rudy was able to get a heavy rope from his barn and we tied it to the ring in front of the boat and dragged it home. It may have been water soaked because it was heavy. We thought of it as a sign it was well made. The three of us came up with ideas as we were fixing our prize, like covering the boards first with tar paper, then shingles. This would waterproof the boat. We knew we never could compete with a Magnum Marine or Noah, because we didn't want to build a lot of boats or a gigantic one, just a good one. The three of us played hooky, deciding one spring day to launch the boat that we Christened with Kool-Aid and named Dobby. Huffing and puffing our way through fields and woods, we finally arrived at the river's bank. We were so excited building a boat that was ours to keep at such young ages.   Carefully, we lowered the boat in the water and one by one we got in. At first we took on a little water, then more and more. The water was not coming through the bottom we protected so well with tar paper and shingles over wood, but was instead seeping through the sides. Thinking back, the boat was probably water soaked, then dried out in the barn and cracked. We watched our dream sink, but since it was such a nice day we stayed to fish, catching many nice sized ones. Rudy said it was a shame after the three of us worked almost four months. He laughed out loud when I said, "Just think, we have the first submarine in the Midwest." Ma Daly told the principle who called, that she kept Mike and me home to get things ready for the spring garden. When Rudy's mom was called, she said Rudy had gone in his new boat to catch fish. When the principle identified herself saying, "You mean Rudy skipped school?" In her broken Hungarian-English she came right back with, "Oh I thought you meant our big boy Frankie. So sorry, but Rudy is in bed with the terrible 'punies'."

Spending time with the Chatterettes

Some time had passed and it was Daly's turn to host the Chatterettes to play Euchre and have dinner. The Chatterettes were a group of maids from work at General Industries where both Loretta and Jane worked. We all stayed home to paint, rake leaves, and clean the house. We were told often that they had permission from the social worker to keep us home from school three or four days a month to work on the farm. After an exhausting day of work Loretta gave me a final job to bury this 10-12 pound fish from the river, the neighbors had dropped off a month or so ago. It hadn't looked good but was put in the freezer anyway. The plan was to make room for a pig they were going to kill in a week or so. Before the group came over, Jane made a small fire in the center of a circle of stones and we cut some willow branches to roast wieners (these were the same branches I had to cut and bring to the basement when I was getting whipped). Loretta and Jane were putting on a good show for the ladies who would be coming shortly. After eating, Loretta brought out some marshmallows and each of us put four or five of them on a stick and placed them over the red hot coals. Suddenly mine caught on fire and I flipped them back quickly with three nice gooey ones landing in Jane's hair. I roared laughing and so did the other kids because she was all dolled up in her best hairdo from the beauty parlor. Jane said she would get to me later and I was to mark those words. How on earth do you mark words, I thought. The Chatterettes were starting to arrive and Jane ran in the house to get the mess out of her hair. I was still laughing as the gals came and one of them said, "You seem to be having such a fun day." This was only the beginning of a long night. Everyone went inside so Mike and I doused the small fire, and headed for the basement.

It was getting chilly out anyway. While the club of ladies were all settled upstairs and having dinner after a drink or two, Mike reminded me about burying the fish. He suggested a plan that I thought was brilliant. Why go back outside when you could just toss it in the furnace? The furnace was well stocked with hickory and oak we had cut during the summer and it didn't take long for the flames to engulf the fish. One by one I could hear the guests saying through the vents, "Do you smell something?" or, "It smells fishy." Next thing I know Loretta barks out, "Lynn, you get up here now!" Often, I have wondered why they would accuse me first, but then again most of the time I was at the root of the problem. I was in deep trouble now! After I explained, Jane pushed me aside and ran downstairs to get the charred fish out of the furnace. She took the shovel we used to clean out the ashes, got the fish and tossed it on the grass outside. I was shooed upstairs to my bedroom only to find out I could listen to the gossip through the heat vent. We had a chamber pot and lid in case we needed it during the night. It was in my way of hearing everything being said so I scooted it away to hear who was going with whom and their other chatter. After about 45 minutes I got up yawning and tripped over the pot sending it clanging down the stairs into the kitchen where four of the gals were playing cards. I came downstairs in my pajamas to gather up the noise maker only to be aware of the amusement on their faces. Saturday, the next day, I was reminded of my shenanigans and had to select a willow branch. At the last minute Loretta said she had a yardstick to use instead. I had to bend over a chair where I took about 15 whacks. My rear end must have been used to this kind of thing, since I faked oohs and aahs. It really didn't hurt that much. Whatever pain there was, it was worth the laughs. This wouldn't be the last of my encounters with the Chatterettes.

The next occasion was one of the first ball games of the season with the Cleveland Indians playing some team I have forgotten. All the Chatterettes were excited that Bob Feller was pitching. I was bored to death with thirty Chatterettes from all over the city. Being the only male on the bus and sitting in the middle they would ruffle my hair, pat me and say what a handsome good looking boy I was. Loretta would pop up and say, don't say that, he already struts around like he owns the world and sometimes I have to take him down a peg or two. No kidding! Now the singing started. First there was the inevitable, <u>Take Me Out to the Ball Game,</u> followed by <u>Happy Birthday,</u> for Lucille, then <u>On Top of Old Smoky</u>, and the worst, <u>100 Bottles of Beer on the Wall</u>. One of the gals tapped me on the shoulder and asked if I had a favorite song. My answer got a few giggles when I said, "Why don't all of you get quiet and enjoy the ride." This "treat" to the ball game was Jane's idea after coming home in a terrible snow storm last winter to find me almost finished shoveling the driveway. With the house sitting on a hill, the driveway was about fifty feet long. Mike was with Loretta and Jane because he was allowed to play basketball, even though he never made the team. I had the talent but was not offered the opportunity to play except for a very occasional time. Jane rolled down her window at the bottom of the hill and said "Good job Lynn, I won't forget this and someday I will surprise you for your hard work, especially this." The surprise was the ball game. When we got to the stadium which seemed to take forever, some would buy programs to share with others. Imagine sitting all together, thirty of them and one of me. Since they had sandwiches and chips on the bus, there was no need to buy food, instead they passed flasks of liquor back and forth. To me baseball was boring with a ball one, strike one, ball two, the wind up, scratch-scratch, spit-spit, ball three etcetera. After several hours of what felt like torture, I think Cleveland won, one to nothing. I don't know if there was any singing on the way home because I slept all the way, in fact I started dozing after the 7th inning stretch.

CARLISLE HELPERS 4-H CLUB

The 4-H club for rural children was an excellent way to learn about specific farm experiences like, the care, feeding, and showing of animals. It also allowed us to have the opportunity to meet and compete with others at the county fair. I started 4-H with the Carlisle Helpers and my sister Dolly was with the Sewing Sally's. The girls could have canning displays and sewing if they chose, or as Dolly elected, they could show animals. She won every year showing Shropshire sheep. At first, I didn't fare as well. My first year was about getting acquainted with the other kids, their animals and all the things the club offered. We met every other week and the meetings were very informative except for the one on tractor maintenance. I found the conversation about gear ratio, power take-off, spark plugs, and oil and gas requirements to be boring. I closed my eyes and ears on most of this stuff, but appeared mildly interested in the topic of air-filters, the last area of discussion. I sat there nodding my head, asking a question and applauded when the instructor finally finished. Normally being asked to be on the Saturday radio show, "Farm House" would be a thrill and honor to most. I was told I was elected and the discussion would be random at the host's discretion and would last about three to five minutes. My worst dream came true when the farm show host introduced me as the youngest in the Carlisle Helpers 4-H club. I was feeling pretty important now, but then he asked me to explain to the listening audience the purpose of the air filter on the tractor. Evidently he was in contact with our club leader who mentioned this was the subject of our last meeting. I took a deep breath then repeated the question as we learned in spelling bee contests in school. I actually was trying to kill time and was squirming a bit because I did not have the full details on the purpose of how the air filter worked. I nervously blurted out how everyone out there knows how dusty and dirty it can be especially when it is dry and hot and the farmer is going fast. I continue with, "You don't see any farmers wearing white face masks with a band around their head because they are a proud bunch. And besides they don't need to." I talked slowly into the mike and figured I had used half of my time already. "You see with the air filter the air comes in, circulates around and the dust and particles are automatically removed." The host held up one finger indicating I guess I had one minute left. I went on to say all the air the farmer is breathing is fresher and cleaner due to this device called the air filter. Finally, I told everyone, "If any of you out there listening don't have one, you should for health reasons. Please check with your Farm Bureau or other farm stores. Thank you for listening to me and have a good day." The radio host said, "Oh my, that was some information and you are quite a nice young lad in a fine organization." I thanked him, bowed although no one else was around and rode my bike home. Some of the neighbors at church told Daly's loud enough so I could hear that I had a way of saying things and someday could be a radio announcer.

Bruno was a Hereford steer (castrated male used for feeding rather than breeding purposes) and was purchased from a cattle dealer. I think they were given a limit to bid on a calf in the auction for me to raise. Bruno was lanky, shy and never filled out like the other kids calves. Some of the other steers were blocky and their stomachs were only eight to ten inches off the ground whereas you could do the limbo and get under mine easily. At the bi-monthly meetings we learned about feeding and grooming techniques and keys to walking and parading your steer before the judges. The months passed quickly and soon the Lorain County Fair arrived. I stayed at the fair all three days and slept each night in the barn next to Bruno. During the day I practiced one of the grooming methods I had learned, like holding the tail up and brushing down to give a fuller look to the rump area. Next was brushing the hair on the hinds inside to out again to give a blockier appearance. Finally it was time for the curry comb, making circles on the calf's coat after linseed oil was applied. I practiced twice a day walking Bruno slowly and lifted the strap from his halter as if the judge was coming by and gently with a cane, rubbed Bruno's underside to calm his nerves. About 11am the day of the competition the Daly's showed up with white pants, a homemade white shirt which looked like a woman's blouse, and six holy medals to pin on my shirt. There was St. Christopher, St. Theresa, St. Luke, St. Joseph, St. Thomas, and St. Peter. These were medals they had accumulated over the years and had them put away for what they considered an important occasion. They even handed me a Blessed Virgin Mary bracelet. I was like a walking saint who just happened to be at the fair to show off a calf. About eighteen or twenty calves were paraded in front of the grandstand and the judges would weave in and out and eventually tap the first place, then second, and so on. This is how we were to line up. When I was tapped I followed what seemed to be a very long line. When we were in our places, the judge would announce the champion and reserve champion. I curiously turned around to see who was behind me, although I already knew the answer, no one was behind me. I had captured last place despite being adorned with holy things. That was okay, I had done the best with what I was given. I later cried because I knew Bruno was auctioned off and would be going to Herman's Slaughter House in Oberlin. Herman saw me crying, put his hand on my shoulder and said, "It's going to be alright kid." He thought I was crying because I came in last. Herman knew the Daly's and my plight so when they came by, he said quite emphatically that he would select a calf for me so I would have a good chance next year. In September a trailer came with a short horn steer and after helping unload him I knew I had a chance to compete. The shorthorn breed is noted for gaining weight fast and this stocky, short legged, reddish brown and white calf had winner written all over his face; I named him Stadler. As the months flew by he grew rapidly and his coat was healthy and shiny from the soy bean oil mixed with molasses in his daily feed. One month before the fair, my pride and joy was mysteriously let out of his pen into the lush alfalfa. He must have gorged himself. When I came home from work I saw my Stadler lying on the ground with a large bloated stomach. My brother Mike had always been jealous of my popularity at school, happy-go-lucky attitude and now a good chance to have the champion steer. He was laughing as I was sobbing. The vet said my calf would be alright, but it would be almost a week with restricted feed before he was back to normal. At the fair, I groomed him and guarded him faithfully readying him for the big day. I did all the things I learned and had done the previous year but this time I didn't need the groves of metals for help. I didn't get awarded Grand Champion, but came in second for the Reserve Champion ribbon. As a calf Stadler weighed 386 pounds on September 15th and on the day of the final weigh in August 25th he tipped the scales at 1157 pounds. This gave him a daily rate gain of slightly over 2.2 pounds, placing him second by only a fraction. I never confronted Mike knowing very well the outcome was not in my favor and could have been a very serious mistake.

A year later, through 4-H, I was selected with just a few other boys from the state to be a guest at The Ohio State University. We toured the campus, and the various agricultural buildings. At dinner we ate with students and were encouraged to ask questions about college life. Although it was 4 years away, I didn't have to be encouraged to go to college; I was going! The four H's represent the head, heart, health, and hands. 4-H has a strong base in project work in which youth acquire knowledge (head), development of the heart is stressed through community service and leadership activities as youth learn to care and share with others, enhance the physical mental and social youth (health), and help others help themselves with their skills (hands). It would be remiss if I didn't say the 4-H pledge!

I pledge:

My head to clearer thinking

My heart to greater loyalty

My hands to larger service and

My health to better living

For my club, my community and my country.

It was my sophomore year in high school and the nuns in the school asked for volunteers to talk about hobbies, clubs, or organizations. I signed up right away to talk about my achievement in going from last place to reserve champion in the 4-H club at the county fair. All of the other kids that agreed to talk to the assembly of students were from the city and I just knew my story would be exciting and I could hardly wait to tell it. I followed a few students who talked about sports, scouts, church groups and charity events in which they were involved. It was my turn. I hadn't had time to rehearse and just talked from real time experience, giving a full detailed account of going from last place to reserve champion in class plus weight gain. I concluded my speech by saying I could have given up, but just dug a little deeper to see how I could improve so that I could reach my goal. Each of us can do this. Set your goals, it is important! Do some research to find out how to achieve them and remember . . .

The greatest danger for most of us isn't that we aim high
and miss it, but we aim too low and reach it
— Michelangelo

MAX VERSUS LYNN

No, it wasn't a threat against my brother Mike who would bite my hands until they were raw. This threat was against Max, the black Minorca Rooster. He was the King around the "hin" house, and stationed himself about half way between the chicken coop and the outhouse. Any time I would go down the path to either place, he would flap those big wings at my face, jump up and peck at me, or chase me. This guard was about three years old when he started his orneriness, and I'd had enough. Over a period of time and what seemed like forty bouts, I decided to make a lasting impression on this bully, one day. From the bread-box I got a large crust from the homemade bread and soaked it in a Stroh's beer that was in the basement. Next I cut the bread in small squares and tossed them to Max. He gobbled down the whole crust and was trying to run but fell down, got up and fell again. I crept up on him with a broom, placed my foot on him and saw his eyes rolling back in his head. Pulling on his big red wattle, I said don't you dare bite or chase me again and I swatted him in the rear. From that time on, my trips by him carrying the broom were trouble free. Max would see me, let out a little crow and stay where he was. Maybe Max was bad because he was a bachelor and all the good-looking chicks were alone in the "hin" house.

HAIR BE GONE

Ma Daly could be a kind soul and would laugh when I made up a song or poem. I will always remember the notes she would write on toilet paper, a brown bag or whatever was handy when I needed a haircut. All students needed permission to leave school during their lunch hour. She would write:

> Dear Nice Sister Lady,
>
> Please excuse Lynn for he has to go to the hair barber to get a haircut.
>
> God Bless You,
>
> Anna Daly

I was always asked to get the note back if possible to save writing another one next time.

How could I forget the times Anna cut my hair. The hair at least wasn't down to the back of my neck anymore, but it was trimmed halfway up from my ears to the top of my head. When I started earning money I paid for my own haircuts. Frances (a foster sister) did not fare so well one time. Anna (or as we called her, Ma) was cutting her hair in the granary. A big zinger of lightning followed by a thunderous boom scared the daylights out of both of them. Ma yelled in fright and then said, 'Whoops!' as she cut a three inch swath right in the middle of Frances's hair. Poor Frances asked me if she looked bad. I said, "I can't lie, but it is pretty bad." She wore a hat to school, rarely taking it off. The rare occasion she did was when she asked me almost daily if her hair had grown out yet.

On my previous trip to the barber, while waiting for a haircut, I noticed in a magazine a new style for men that was catching on in California…the fashion state. The picture was of a crew-cut where your hair was straight up and squared off. I told my friends at school and they dared me to get mine cut that way. I told them to make it worth my while so nickels, dime, pennies, and even a couple quarters were raised for a total of $1.38. I showed the picture to the barber and he said he had never done one before, but he would try. My crew-cut was about three inches tall, waxed and combed straight up. After lunch when I returned to school the class roared with laughter. The nuns were quite upset with the commotion and I became the talk of the P.T.A. The nuns really couldn't say much other than to stop staring and laughing. After all, it wasn't even a venial sin.

What was that Brown Furry Thing?

In the fall we spent more than the allocated three or four days a month home to paint, bale hay, cut wood, or husk corn. After all this was the free days from school the Daly's were allowed to keep us home. It was normally late September or October when the field corn was ready for husking. Now mind you, in early August when the ears were quite young, the eating was fine…not quite like sweet corn, but it was corn and food. When the field corn was dry enough to husk, all the kids would take a row or one side and toss the ears to an area where later the tractor and trailer would slowly go up and down as we tossed the ears again. One time, because I liked it and I was fast at husking corn, I went out on my own to get more harvested. At dinner I told of seeing a brown furry something and Ma Daly said right away it was the devil. Imagine that! I went upstairs to my holy box (another band-aid can) and got out the holy scapular. The nuns had told us that if you wore this cloth piece you would not suffer eternal fire if you died. I didn't wear it much. When I first got it I did and I would wake up choking with one side around my neck and the other around my waistline. Figuring I probably would live a long life, I had put the scapular in with the other holy medals and rosary and just got it out on days when it was needed. You know, if the priest was giving me the last rites, I would pop up and say pardon me Father, but I really need the scapular to scare off the devil and get into heaven. Now, back to husking corn . . . again, I went out on my own to surprise Ma Daly. This time I took the scapular with me. I even put it on the outside of my shirt so the devil could see it and not tempt me with bad thoughts or laziness. It worked! No devil, no temptations or bad thoughts and lots of nice ears of corn. I was happy and thought of all the ears of corn grinning at me. I saw the checkered shirt on the clothesline that was a sign to come home for dinner. Wish we had a dinner bell!

A Phantom at Our House

At the foster home I remember only once when Loretta showed some kindness or likeness to a human being. She had gone to Dr. Sullivan several times and all Jane would say is she had some female problem. She was scheduled to go to the hospital for a double mastectomy. The best way Jane could explain it to me was she had a bad case of mastitis. On the day of Loretta's surgery, I walked her to the car and opened the door for her. She turned, patted me on the head, and got in. I could see her crying as she waved good-bye to me with her hankie. Loretta died at a fairly early age, in her late sixties and even now I remember her in my evening prayers.

That forgiveness has begun when you recall those that
hurt you and feel the power to wish them well
– Lewis B. Smedes

DAY TO DAY LIVING

One of the things the Lord hates is a heart that devises wicked plans
and one who sows discord among other people
– Proverbs 6:16

A BIRTHDATE FOR ME

The day that Marlene brought my Uncle Bill, Aunt Jeanette, and Grandmother Eula, all of whom I had never met before, to the Daly's house was the same day that Marlene whispered to me, "I know that you were born November 14, 1939". I knew all along it was some time in the fall but now I knew the exact date.

I thought when my grandma, Eula, went directly into the Daly's forbidden sanctuary of the living room that she had spunk. This was the room we were never ever allowed to enter. Lamp shades, chairs, and the sofa were covered with plastic, which were taken off once or twice a year when the Chatterettes came to play euchre or for special guests. My grandma must have not been considered special since all the plasticized furniture stayed as it was.

She was a rough, coyote-shooting lady from Wyoming who spoke what was on her mind. When she plunked down in one of the over-stuffed chairs and the plastic rattled, she said to me, "Come here you little rascal so I can see you better". It was strange and difficult for me to cross the psychological electric fence that divided the dining room from the living room. At first I hesitated, looked around for approval, and then entered. I nervously patted grandma's hand, said hi, and ran out. I did not want to stay in the living room too long and take the consequences later from my foster family. Not understanding the circumstances, grandma said, "You sure are a fine looking boy, but you are so bashful".

Signs of Spring in the Midwest

What goes around comes around, sometimes even counter clockwise. I was sitting on the edge of the porch watching this gray-black funnel cloud maybe a couple miles away. I didn't know the exact distance, but it had not reached the woods yet which was several hundred yards away. You could hear a chicken laying an egg it was so quiet. Everyone was outside and the wind picked up a little, then a little more. As we all ran in the house just in time, Loretta, Jane, Ma Daly, Mike and I struggled to close the door behind us. The swirling tornado was tossing everything in its path. The outhouse tipped over, boards on the porch were flying off, shingles from the roof were falling to the ground, and most of the chicken coop windows sounded like small explosions as they broke. Before we could get the door shut, quite a few windows in the house shattered and glass was all over. A large walnut tree by the milk house was uprooted and the 50 gallon gas tank was picked up and deposited across the road. A rake, shovel, scythe, broom, and a pitchfork were flung through the air like arrows shot from a bow. What seemed like hours was really only about four to five minutes. Suddenly it was quiet and I walked outside into the wind blown wet alfalfa field and said, "Thank you God. It could have been worse, but thanks for giving them a wakeup call."

THE SINS OF POETRY

We were asked to write a poem of our choosing in the sixth grade. Living on a farm and having nature all around, it was an easy and fun assignment. I wrote:

Swiftly down the flooded creek the old oak floats,

Like the coming of tugs, barges and other boats

Frogs a croaking, birds all singing

New grass, plants and buds springing

Pheasants in their multi-colored vests

Strut down rows of stalks showing off their best

Little wooly lambs are bouncing and bleating

Our feathered friends make music tweeting

It is spring time for sure, just smell the air

The calves, lambs and piglets don't have a care

New born squirrels scamper up and down the tree

While baby bunnies run zigzag, saying mother catch me

Worms wiggle up both day and night

While Robins pounce softly with delight

Their feet would patter up and down like rain

So when the worm came out, oh, what a strain

All this would happen and all too soon

With the best seat to watch all, the silvery moon.

The Sister graded my poem with a "D" and put a note on my paper
. . . plagiarism is a sin!

What a contradiction when I was told by the same woman that she thought I had talent. "You are talented and could be another Robert Frost." She related how he wrote a classic yet simple phrase, "The fog comes in on little cat paws. It sits looking over harbor and city on haunches then moves on."

A Revealing Experience

We cut most of our firewood during the summer, put it into high piles and transported to the barn by sled or pulled with a wagon. During the summer there wasn't a need for socks or underwear, in fact this was the general rule from May through October for me. On one particularly warm summer morning I was on the other end of a cross-cut saw with Anna "Ma" Daly. This was a busy time of year, like the squirrels stash their berries, apples and corn, we stashed firewood. While sawing, pushing the blade back and forth, my innocent little pee pee sneaked out of a tear in the crotch of my bib overalls and was swinging in the wind back and forth with the sawing motion. Ma Daly stopped and said, "You should tuck that back in your pants because many people get arrested for showing something like that in public." I told her, "I didn't know it was out because being warm outside, it felt just as though it was in." This really slowed us down since I had become self conscious and had to keep checking so that I didn't get reported and put in jail.

Sex Lessons Were a Lot of Bull

The nuns either didn't know how to teach sex or they were embarrassed to talk about it. It was the eighth grade and the girls were sprouting their wings and the guys were keenly aware they were different.

Now at the Daly's with no man around to discuss the subject they had the ideal answer. When Rosie, the lead cow went in heat, they told me to lead her to the neighbor's farm where they had other cows and one or two bulls. As I led Rosie past the gate the head bull came swinging towards us with his nostrils flaring, snorting and hoofing dirt along the way. He quickly came over and mounted Rosie, before long he was down and it was over. Rosie's eyes were really big like she just got a surprise and after a bit we headed back to the barn. When I returned to the house both Loretta and Jane had this big smirk on their faces. "Well, what did you see and what do you think, huh?" They kept teasing me as they knew I was blushing. "Did you see the bull's big thing?" I wanted to leave the kitchen, but dinner was almost ready. They kept going, "Lotta turning, grinding and fast action, don't you think?" I never commented figuring I had done what I had been asked and after dinner went to the barn to tell Rosie that she was special and precious. I was so happy she wasn't hurt by that big bully.

A FISH STORY

In my mind, opportunity didn't have to knock, the door was always open and she was free to come in anytime. The city of Elyria was sponsoring a fishing contest in the park pool, all kids age eight to twelve were invited with various prizes offered for their catch. The water was crystal clear and you could see many fish swimming around. During my lunch break I asked one of my friends who lived close by if I could borrow his fishing gear. Not having any bait, I decided there were enough fish so that maybe I could just snag a big one. My friend Chet told me there was a large carp gasping on the bottom right by the drain. I lowered my line and after several attempts hooked this lunker. We both ran with excitement to the nearby weight station to see how big it was. It tipped the scale at eight pounds, twelve ounces, making me the winner. The next day my name was in the paper for catching the biggest fish. The prize was three silver dollars. I gave one to Chet, saved one for the church collection and hid one in a band-aid can in the basement.

NOT MY HIGH SCHOOL HANG-OUT

Many of my classmates would migrate to the Paradise Restaurant where Harry would serve Cokes and sundaes after school. The buzzing was about who liked who, and who was going with who and such stuff. When I wasn't in detention or hitch-hiking home, I was working somewhere so I had little free time. One time though, I did go to the Paradise, figuring I wouldn't look like a snob, besides, I just had to see this hangout that I had heard so much about. What a let-down! As at the dances, most of the girls were by themselves and the boys were seated separately or standing. There was the occasional couple who was going steady, sitting together. The gals were whispering in each other's ears and giggling and both sexes would comment on new arrivals. Sooner or later Harry would shout out, "Okay, drink up and get out." Most of his clientele would buy one Coke, sipping on it for an hour or so. How absolutely boring! I decided on my first and last visit this was a place that should have been called Harry's Hormone House or the Squirrel's Nest. I never went back.

Songs in My Head

I have always liked country-western music with the strumming guitar notes and mellow tones. Especially what Johnny Cash put forth. They were heart-warming and always had a message. His Folsom Prison Blues was a good song, but the beat to I've Been Everywhere was special to me with my travels. Just hear a portion of the lyrics:

I've been everywhere, man, I've been everywhere,, man . . .

Been to Reno, Chicago, Fargo, Minnesota, Buffalo, Toronto, Winslow, Sarasota, Wichita, Tulsa, Ottawa, Oklahoma, Tampa, Panama, Mattawa, La Paloma, Bangor, Baltimore, Salvador, Amarillo, Tocapillo, Baranquilla, and Perdilla . . .

I've been everywhere, man, I've been everywhere, man . . .

Although I have not been everywhere, a song could be written on my illnesses and injuries growing up and today.

I've had many a thump man, I've had many a thump man . . .

Parasites, Intestinal Worms, Ring Worm, Tape Worm, Scarlet Fever, Head Lice, Pneumonia four times, Mal Nutrition, Mumps, Measles, Chicken Pox . . .

I've had a few more things man, I've had a few more things man . . .

Broken Ankle, Ruptured Appendix, Broken Leg, Broken Arm, Double Hernia, Bells Palsy . . .

I've had a few more thumps man, I've had a few more thumps man . . . Two knee replacements, a staph infection in the same knee, two hand surgeries for Dupuytren's contraction, and now a scheduled rotator cuff repair.

Our "Hin" House
Made the Grade

In a general science class we had in the eighth grade we were studying birds or ornithology as Sister called it. There was a lot of discussion on different kinds of birds, colors, nesting habits and feeding areas. We had several pages of material that Sister Monica passed out. Later we had a short exam on the material. We were all assigned a project to write our own paper, take pictures or do whatever we wanted. The three weeks given to complete the project that represented 85% of our grade was more than enough time for me. With the help from a book in the library and access to lots of feathers from the "hin" house, I was more than ready for the task. First I collected feathers from the coop and around the yard, then looked for similar feathers on the birds in the book.

A white leghorn chicken feather looked similar to an egret, seagull and swan, whereas the black Minorca chicken feathers gave me a crow, and blackbird. The guinea fowl was a great find as I matched her plumage to grey heron, dark eyed junco and spotted owl. At first I hesitated with a baby chick's yellow fuzz but pasted in beneath the name finch. The Rhode Island's smaller red feathers could be called a robin and the larger, darker ones matched with a golden eagle. The little unknown buckeye complimented the red bellied woodpecker and scarlet tanager. I got an A+ and three silver stars with a note stating outstanding, creative and original. I believe when I got my project back on the birds, there were several lice crawling around the page. I was asked to share my report to the class and after much clapping and cheering I knew I had center stage so I asked the kids if they had ever watched a robin after it rains. I told them he pounces on the grass as if it is still raining and when the worm peeks out he nabs it. They all laughed and I heard a few saying they had noticed that before too.

*"Creative minds have always been known to
survive any kind of bad training"*
— Anna Freud

ME, RESPONSIBLE FOR A
GRAND CANYON?

Each spring the creek would flood the pasture, go over its banks and sometimes even over the bridge. It was fun to see the muskrats scurrying to higher ground and the frogs and turtles awakening from their winter nap. Several times in the fourth and fifth grade when I was ten and eleven, I would bring a shovel and dig a trench diverting the creek. I had seen a picture of the Grand Canyon in a book and thought maybe if enough water flowed through the channel, in 50 million years I could be responsible for another spectacular gorge. No wonder the nuns at school said I had a very vivid imagination. I told my story in geography class and most of the kids were nodding in agreement and quite a few said wow. Sister Michael must have felt I was on to something too because she asked me to come to the blackboard and write out how I saw my small ditch grow to be something so big. My theory was just a one one-hundreth of an inch a year would increase to ten inches deep in 1,000 years and 500,000 inches or approximately seven and one-half miles in 50 million years. Now the width could be ten to twelve miles. I wish you could have heard the ooh's and aah's. I never watched the progression of that small trench I made because I learned with nature you had to be patient. No doubt I would live to be 100, but the depth would have increased only one inch. The two times in college I came back to the Daly's I never looked at the creek as I drove over, but had to laugh inwardly at my future optimism as a scrawny kid growing up. My goals were high, but attainable since I firmly believed in them. Long before Michael Jordan, Kobe Bryant, or Lebron James, I would often dream of floating twenty feet from the basket and way above it, just dropping the ball in the hoop. I may not have had much, but I did much with the big dreams I had.

In taking revenge, a man is but even with his enemy,
but in passing it over, he is superior
- Frances Bacon

A Garden In My Pocket

At the end of the seventh grade Sister Michael said there would be a contest during the summer to see how many books we read. I would hitch-hike to the library in Elyria and bring back a bag full of books at a time. Most of the books were autobiographies and included Patton, Grant, Lincoln, Miles Standish, Captain Farragut, Nathan Hale and Geronimo to name a few. There is a Chinese Proverb, "A book is like a garden carried in the pocket." When I wasn't doing the daily chores, cutting grass, weeding the garden and carrying wood, there was time to put the cows in an adjourning five acres where the grass was very lush. I would prop up against a tree and read. Sometimes I fell asleep only to be awakened by the lead cow Rosie licking my face and hair. She was trying to tell me the other cows, Marty (the Holstein), and Polly and Molly (twin Swiss) were crossing the road. I would shoo them back and continue reading. In September, back at school I had reported reading seventeen books during the summer break and was by far the winner in the class.

A First Kiss

It was at our 25th high school class reunion in 1982, when Diane introduced me to her husband and said, "This was my boyfriend in high school." It was then, that I recalled my first kiss.

To most, this would not be a big issue, but I do not remember ever being kissed, hugged, or greeted with a good-morning, good night, or wished a happy birthday while growing up. It was March, in the eighth grade and Mary Jo was having a spring party. I was so excited that I could not even make a basket hit the rim on the side of the barn thinking how I was going to tell Diane my secret. The party was a week away and I was thinking of writing a note to Diane asking if maybe at the party we could step outside or in one of the rooms because I would like to offer her my first kiss. I even told the pigs, calves, lambs, kittens, and chickens because I knew they could keep a secret. I thought twice about writing a note thinking that if nosy Loretta found out she would laugh and that would be so embarrassing. I came so close the day before the party but figured I would just whisper to Diane when nobody was around.

At the party, there were lots of games, laughing, ice cream and cookies. Time flew and before I knew it Loretta was hobbling across the yard toward the front door. By the time she had reached the door, I had already thanked everyone, put on my coat and hat and was out the door. My second chance for a kiss would not be until October when I stayed after school to play basketball. This was one of the few times I had given myself such a treat. Diane was watching me practice and afterwards I walked her home. She invited me in and after meeting her parents we went to her room. Ever since that "almost" day in March I was concerned about my larger nose than her pug. It wasn't that my nose and even ears were so big, it was that my face was so thin. I thought face to face I could miss her mouth because no doubt there would be a gap. Next, I thought of turning sideways, closing my eyes and just aiming, but I could miss and only hit the side of her mouth. Now was the moment of truth and declaration. I made sure the door was closed tightly, held Diane's face in my hands, and kissed her right smack on the center of her mouth. Wow, oh boy! I felt as though I had left earth and was floating in the sky. I thought to myself, no wonder people get married, they can do this all the time. She unbuttoned her blouse just at the neck. I really think I gave her a hot spasm or something. We smiled at each other, left the room and her parents invited me to stay for dinner. They were having meatloaf, mashed potatoes, green beans and red Jell-O with real whipped cream. I thanked them and said I really should be going now. Diane walked with me a half block or so and then decided to turn back. I walked her back because it was dark and I wanted her to be safe. After a short distance her parents pulled up and offered me a ride to the outskirts of town. I assured them I could easily hitch a ride from there. Getting out of the car, I squeezed Diane's hand, smiled, waved, thanked them and wished them all a good night. I could have skipped all the way but after just two rides I arrived home. Jane asked where in the heck I was and pointed at the clock, it was 7:15pm. Now it was Loretta's turn. Are you sensing a tag team at its finest? We were about to call the sheriff on you and report you missing or abducted. I said, "Sorry, I played basketball, lost track of time and had to walk most of the way home." "No damn excuse you worthless fool," said Loretta. "You are going to bed without dinner and mark my words, someday you will learn to obey. I accepted my punishment because although my stomach was growling and I passed up a dinner in the city, it was very, very much worth it. I was smiling inside and out and was full of excitement and happiness. I did it, I did it, and fell fast asleep.

Happiness is like a kiss – it feels better when you give it to someone else.
– Anonymous

An Angel in My Lunch

When I was thirteen, sisters Frances and Betty came to live at the Daly's. Frances was my age and Betty was a year younger. One day, Frances and I recorded our height with a mark inside the chicken coop. We then got a ruler to see how tall we were and added our weight. I was 5'3" tall and weighed 87 pounds and she was 5'1" tall, weighing 104 pounds. I figured that Frances had sprouting female parts that gave her the advantage. At school my nickname was "Bones". I knew I was skinny and so did all of my classmates. Soon after we measured ourselves, Loretta and Jane took me to their Dr. Sullivan, Irish of course, who also measured and weighed me. This was the first and only time I had been to a doctor for a physical although I had been sick a lot. The only question Dr. Sullivan asked me, with his southern Irish accent, was if my bowels moved. Later I figured he meant bowls, but at the time of questioning I said, "Oh yes, especially when I run or walk fast." He asked me to wait in another room and I could hear him say, "This kid has mal-nutrition and at this growth state you have to feed him better." A few weeks later, after an intramural basketball game that my foster caregivers came to, Jane was commenting to Loretta on the way home, "My God, in comparison to the other kids, he really is skinny."

The next fall, Carol, a girl sitting next to me "forgot" her lunch money so I offered to share my large, thick cut homemade sandwich and apple. I gave the sandwich to her and asked if she would divide it. This was the first few days of school in September and there were still plenty of vegetables in the garden. Carol opened the sandwich and said, "Oh my, they forgot the meat." Although the sandwiches had gotten better after going to the doctor, I never had meat on a sandwich. This day it was lettuce with sliced vegetables and a large apple I had plucked from the neighbor's tree, with permission, of course. Carol's mother was a volunteer nurse at the school and her dad was a very successful doctor. Looking back, I believe she had Carol deliberately forget her lunch money to see what kind of nutrition I was getting. It wasn't long afterwards that Mike, Dolly, and I all received an envelope from our teachers that had a pink card entitling us to free cafeteria food. This angel had done a wonderful thing as it used to be a long time between our meager meals. Sometimes my stomach hurt from hunger and I would take a can of Hershey Syrup from the basement shelf, puncture it, drink some and hide the rest. My other stash of goods included jam, peanut butter, or canned fruit. This was usually after the vegetables in the garden no longer were able to produce because of frost. With the free school lunch passes, I did start to gain weight. It helped too, that I started drinking about a pint of cream right from the milk house each day.

Earning Money

I had only been back to school a few weeks when Ann Piazza asked me if I knew anyone who would like to work on her dad's produce farm. I couldn't say I would fast enough, but had to check at home and get back to her in the morning. I was so excited to get a real job paying real money that I hitch-hiked home to beat the bus, beating it by forty-five minutes. I knew this from having to stay after school for detentions which lasted about a half hour. The Daly's never suspected anything until they got my report card with all P's (poor) for conduct and thirteen detentions.

Ma Daly said I could accept the job as long as I still did the chores around the house. When Jane and Loretta got home they said yes without even hesitating. I worked an hour or so after school and all day Saturday and Sunday. Many times I would bring my work clothes, boots and shoes to 6am mass on Sunday and get a ride from Piazza's who also attended that early service. I worked as much as I could fit in my schedule with one goal in mind, college.

The local vet was my mentor and I watched him when he would attend the animals. Little did I know that my goal eventually would be challenged and my career and ambition changed for life. At school I volunteered to be a crossing guard after attending a short course during lunch hour on safety at cross-walks. During the year we were treated to free milk, I always took chocolate and at the end of the year we were treated to a Cleveland Indians baseball game. I never did take in the game because it interfered with my work. I even took a Saturday evening job directing cars into parking spots at the Palladium. This was a dance hall our neighbors had built. I usually worked from 7:30 to 9:30 or 10:00pm. For pay I recieved one dollar per hour and could have two hamburgers and a soda.

When I wasn't working on the produce farm or when the hours were short, I helped clean the Palladium. I swept floors, vacuumed the carpet and scrubbed the restrooms. Steve, the owner and my neighbor would give me a ride both ways. I never kept track of the money I made, just handed it over to Loretta as I was told and she would do the banking for me. Talk about a fox guarding the hen house.

During my high school years I worked long and tedious hours. I brought checks home many times for $120-$130 every two weeks. The cast on my ankle and later my leg did not hinder my work habits. I had a walking cast in both cases but my hands were free. Those breaks were in God's plan to slow me down as I was constantly fighting in school and was loud and rebellious. I rebelled because I was asked by the social worker to go to St. Edwards in Cleveland to live, so that I could play football and basketball. Loretta and Jane told them no, as they wanted control so that I would work the farm, and bring in money. I liked basketball and was a natural, I could run football patterns easily as the alfalfa field was my practice arena with my brother arching passes way in front of me. Even the high school football coach, who also taught physical education, sensed my ability to run, pass, and catch and said if I would go out for football he would bring me home after practice and every game. I was not allowed and that hurt. Someone once said, "tears are only sweat that has not been absorbed on the way to victory." I worked steadily at the produce farm and saw quite a few guys that would come to work for a day, maybe a week, and then quit. One guy I will never forget is Ralph. Now Ralph was a lanky good ole boy from the south somewhere. I never asked where he came from, but his accent said south. He was a good worker but his waistline and I.Q. were probably evenly matched. One time we were finished cutting two wagon loads of cabbage that were sitting behind the barn. It was starting to rain and Dominic asked Ralph to cover the cabbage. Ralph was gone several hours and when he came back Dominic asked him where on earth he had been. Ralph told us he had used up all the tarps, bags, newspapers, broken down crates and whatever else he could find to cover the cabbage. He said, "Man, do you know how big that field is?" As realization dawned on us as to what had happened Dominic said, "Holy cow! The wagon loads of cabbage heads, not the eight acre field!"

Piazza Produce entered into the greenhouse business growing mostly geraniums. A truck delivered a large load of peat mixed with sand and just dumped it into a pile. From the pile the dirt had to be brought to a bin where heater cables sterilized the dirt for insects and weeds. Dominic found this very large construction wheel barrow and suggested we heap it up. Then he got a harness for around Ralph's neck and shoulders while I steered with the handles. After Dominic attached the leather straps, Ralph turned to me and said, "I feel like a darn horse." I said, "Why do you say that? Giddy up now, giddy up!" I still laugh when I think of this as well as the other things Ralph did. It made work sometimes fun and easier.

A Salesman at the Door

Living with the Daly's presented many problems but one that made grammar in school difficult was their slaughter of the English language. One wouldn't have to guess how far in school they Daly's had progressed. When Anna's son Clarence came over to fix or build something, they would ask invariably if he "et" yet. One day a load of boys were being trucked to a berry farm and when they passed me out in the yard they shouted out F you. I thought it was some sort of slang and at the end of the day when they were returning, I waved to them and shouted F you. I was overheard by Jane and my ignorance resulted in getting my mouth "wrenched" out with soap and water in the "zink". So that I wouldn't forget, I was asked if I had "brung" the eggs in from the "hin" coop. Two pieces of bread, usually without meat, was called a "samich". The smoke from the burning wood went up the "chimley" and the water we "brung" in from the well was put on the stove to "het" up for our weekly, community baths. Punies....another word for a variety of sickness. It was no wonder that when a salesman knocked at the door and Ma Daly opened it she came out with, "We ain't in the need for nothing." I said to Mike, "How did she know, maybe he was selling English books!" Luckily, I wasn't overheard.

PLASTIC CHICKEN

In 1928, when Herbert Hoover promised, "a chicken in every pot", he didn't mean the oldest or toughest "hin" cooked in a plastic container. It was unusual for Ma Daly, Loretta, and Jane to all be gone at the same time. On this particular day, they had been called by the social worker to meet two more children that needed a home. Since the place was near Cleveland, which was about twenty miles away, they said they would be home late in the afternoon. They planned to stop at Frisch's Big Boy to get their favorite strawberry pie with whipped cream on the way home. We had a whole house full of residents. Carmen, Maria, Roger, Sally, Frances and Betty lived along with Mike, Dolly and me. Frances, bless her heart, said that she wanted to make dinner to surprise the Daly's. On her own, she caught the biggest chicken at about eight pounds, cleaned and dressed it and was preparing it as the main course. Two things happened that rained on her parade. First she caught the largest chicken, thinking that she would need this to feed all of us. Little did she know she had caught the oldest hen that turned out to be very tough. Secondly, in her innocent ignorance, she was baking the chicken in a plastic container and it melted all around the bird. The Daly's came home and immediately opened the oven since they could smell the odor throughout the house. Surprisingly, they never said a word, just tossed the chicken out and said to Frances that it was a good try and an honest mistake. For dinner we had some left over soup from the freezer. They just added some rice. Frances's bottom lip was quivering, realizing that she tried her best to surprise everyone. She left the kitchen and went outside. I followed her saying it was a nice thought and she had nothing to be ashamed of. She looked at me with moist eyes, blinked them, and with a sheepish grin, she thanked me. Later, I thought Frances needed something to cheer her up so I went across the road to pick her a bouquet of wild flowers and put the whole bunch in a Mason pint jar. When I gave them to her, she started to smile and we both sat down on this large tree stump, laughing about the darn big, tough, plastic chicken.

The earth laughs through flowers
– Ralph Waldo Emerson

A CLOSE SHAVE

It was the spring of 1955, my sophomore year in high school, and walking or riding to school I always had to think how clever those Burma Shave signs were. Each time I read one beside the country road, I rubbed my face and thought about starting to shave because the once blonde fuzz on my face was now darker and bristly. A few of the various signs along the way were:

1) The poorest guy in the human race can have a million dollar face. Burma Shave

2) Past schoolhouses take it slow, let a little shaver grow. Burma Shave

3) Train approaching, whistle squealing, avoid that run down feeling. Burma Shave

Every time I got near the railroad tracks I saw that sign.

One day, I decided it was time for me to try shaving. In the basement cabinet over the "zink" was a razor the kind that had a single one edged blade. We didn't have any shaving cream so I lathered well with soap. The blade wasn't very sharp and it was old. I could have pulled my facial hair off with tweezers with less pain. It took me about twenty five minutes to shave and I wasn't bleeding too badly in the end. I did have four band-aids to cover my wounds. The neighbor lady who picked me up for school was covering her face, as I approached her car. She no doubt was concealing a laugh about my first shaving experience. When I got to school none of the kids said anything, although I did get a few casual glances. At recess I peeled off the band-aids, felt my face and decided it wasn't so scratchy. Maybe it wasn't the million dollar face, but it certainly was worth the effort. A health and beauty company should have a package for beginning shavers. It could include the following:

1 razor for double edged blades

6 double edged blades

1 box of band-aids or adhesive strips

1 package of gauze

1 septic pencil

And Yet, Another Broken Bone

The summer between my sophomore and junior year I was guiding the produce truck driver to the loading ramp. He obviously didn't see me in his rearview mirror and kept backing up until he heard what he thought sounded like a basket breaking. It was my arm he had crushed against the building. If I had been over another four inches I would have been crushed to death. Jack, the driver got out of the truck and I crumpled to the ground, sat up and said Jack I think you broke my arm. It seemed like hours at the hospital and I was in their care for several days. It had to be set with a platinum plate and four screws. I sold these in college to a fraternity brother who said he was going to have them melted down for a wedding ring. Although I collected workmen compensation, which I handed over to Loretta, I had a good right arm and I was out of my ankle and leg cast so I had three of my four appendages. The arm definitely slowed me down, I couldn't have played for St. Edwards if I had been allowed to and high school sports were out of the question. Now I wasn't fighting in school and had a quieter demeanor. My new nickname was "Arm" as I had it in a cast for 14 months. When the doctors took off the cast, the diameter of my arm was about the size of a silver dollar. He said the good news was no more cast, but the bad news was I would never use that arm again. I did my own therapy lifting an empty wallet, graduating to carrying empty pails, then ½ lbs weights. It took me almost a year, but I straightened it out. The doctor said it was a miracle.

The happiest people don't have the best of everything, the just make the best of everything they have
- Anonymous

SISTER MICHAEL SHOULD
HAVE EXPECTED THIS

The boys and girls had separate religion classes and one day Sister Michael said we have a surprise visit from a nun from Indianapolis. She had selected Earl, Jake, John, Harry, and me to sit in the front of the class to answer questions directed at us. This was to show our visitor how well we learned from the Bible. Just as a table and five chairs were assembled in front of the class Sister Mary Josephine, our guest, was at the door. After introductions, Sister Michael starter firing questions at the elite whiz kids sitting up front.

Q: "Why did Peter deny that he knew Jesus?"

John - A: "Because he was chicken and figured the cock wouldn't crow anyhow because it was night and they don't crow till morning." Then he lets out a cock a doodle doo!

Earl - A: "He was just saving his hide because there was no way he wanted to get thrashed." He guessed right, the odds were not in his favor.

Q:" Why were there only twelve apostles when more would have been better to spread the word?"

Lynn - A: "The pay was poor, in fact below minimum wage and the boat they fished in could hold just twelve. Besides, with Jesus at the head table at the last supper, it was crowded already."

Jake - A: "Nobody wanted to dress like those dudes...long robes, sandals, no socks, and walking for miles at a time mumbling holy stuff cause their minds were strained from the hot sun."

Sister Michael turned red when everyone laughed.

Q:" Why was John the Baptist so holy and such a leader?"

Harry - A: "He had a secret recipe using sun dried locusts and discovered a special herb he used as cologne. People could smell him coming a mile away and flocked to him."

Earl - A: "He loved dunking people in the river and those locusts gave him gas that he passed just as he was lowering their heads in the water."

Now the class was doubling up and the five of us were giddy. Both nuns were furious! Finally, Sister Michael blurted out, "That's it; this show is over you big hooligans! Shame on all of you, up there in front. I thought I had selected the brightest for our visitor." She walked up to us and shook her finger, scolded and slammed each one of us. "Earl, you are a mockery and disgrace, making the class laugh is a sin when you are discussing the Holy Bible. You owe God an apology and better hope he accepts it. John, you are a spoiled brat and you are a fat nuisance. Someday you will grow up and it won't be too soon. You blubbery good for nothing. Lynn, you could have been the sole leader today, but elected to follow the easy way and side with these renegades. You especially disappointed me." We couldn't control our laughter. You might say we had a jag on. "Jake, you big lug, you might be good at football, but are dumb worth nothing when it comes to the Bible. Why you couldn't even wash the feet of the apostles."

Earl said, "Phew, they probably smelled anyway!" This brought more laughter.

"Harry, although you are 6'6" you are as stupid as you are tall. The apostles may have been short, slight people but Holy."

Sister Michel apologized for the rash of disrespect and later told us we each had three detentions.

The tenth grade was fun, boys were flirting and hormones were abundant as witnessed by the squirreliness of the students. We had a couple dances after school that lasted about an hour and a half and most appeared ideal for the game Red Rover, Red Rover. All the boys were on one side of the gym and the girls on the other. In the game you would call a name and that person had to run and crash through. If not, he or she would have to go back. Cake and punch was served at break time and that was one of the few times there was mingling. Since not much dancing was going on, the president of the class announced the next dance was ladies choice. Some guys lucked out and most danced with the one who did the selecting. The nuns would circulate to make sure there was not too much body contact or pressing of bodies. In health we were told when dancing to keep hands off our partner's neck, as this aroused passions. Sleeveless blouses were a no-no as developing busts were very personal even though they teased boys. Some boys claimed certain girls stuffed tissues in their bras. It was the girls secret, but they were told not to wear patent leather shoes as roving eyes from the boys could catch a glimpse of their underwear.

Just before summer break Sister Giovanni called me into a classroom and with just the two of us made a profound statement that stayed with me and shook me to the bone. She told me I was a gifted, bright, and personable young man with a vivid imagination. She hesitated then staring directly at me said, "Here are your life choices: You have everything you need to be a very successful person or with your carefree and reckless attitude, you could sit in prison for the rest of your life. The choice is yours!" I thanked her and said I would never forget those words and I didn't.

A loving caring teacher took a liking to me. She noticed the potential and wanted to help shape it.
– Tom Bradley

I firmly believe Sister wanted me to visit a seminary in Cleveland, thinking I would make a good priest. For a few short moments I thought about how it certainly would be much better than the conditions I was currently living in but something inside told me to say no, and I relayed my decision. Just a week or so before school started Father Tom came by the house and asked if I would like to go with him on a long weekend to the bowery in Chicago. I was given permission and was quite excited to serve the poor people. Father Tom would pick me up Friday and return me on Monday.

I was given explicit instructions to wear simple clothing and no jewelry. Of course, I didn't have anything to worry about.

At dusk on Friday and Saturday we served soup and sandwiches. The lines were very long. Some of the other volunteers were telling me stories of some of the people who inhabited this jungle in the city. There were doctors, lawyers, bankers and one time successful business people who had fallen out of grace. Perhaps the purpose of my invitation was to make a lasting impression of what could happen to me if I failed to adjust my habits.

Sunday morning we attended mass at St. Sabina's, an African-American Catholic Church on the west side. The music had a great beat and the people were joyous and jubilant. I had never witnessed this before since our parish was quite reserved. The drums, guitar and saxophone playing enticed the congregation to sing and dance their hearts out. I was impressed! We got a few stares at first, but after mass the priest said we were welcome anytime and thanked us for attending.

After a short walk and breakfast we went to Maxwell Street, where vendors had clothing, books, and an assortment of pots, pans, and inexpensive watches and rings. The only things I bought were chartreuse and pink shoe laces and socks which were "in" at the time. Quite a few people had their soap box where they were preaching or playing an instrument with a pan for donations.

We had a light dinner before heading back to the bowery to serve stew and biscuits. William Slocum of Colliers Magazine wrote: "Chicago's near west side hosts one of the jungles of the city. Skid row is like an open jail for men whose only crime may be poverty or loneliness."

I was glad to have had the opportunity to visit and serve the poor and shared my experience with our religion class once school reopened.

We ourselves feel that what we are doing is just a drop in the ocean,
but the ocean would be less because of that missing drop
— Mother Teresa

IF A CAT HAS NINE LIVES, I'VE HAD THIRTEEN

IF A CAT HAS NINE LIVES, I'VE HAD THIRTEEN

It is said a cat has nine lives, but I beat my furry friends by four.

No. 1 – My first and only bicycle was purchased for $2.50, and had no fenders or chain guard. Jane painted it a Kelly green (Irish of course). It wasn't nearly as nice as the maroon, thinner-tired, brand new bike my brother got. His came with the new freezer and I was told again, that he got it because he was older than me. I was happy with my bike anyway, and one day asked if I could ride it to the store, about five miles away to get a newspaper. Along my ride, I misjudged the distance of a truck coming down Route 10. I pedaled across the county road and a trucker blasted and blasted his horn, just missing me by a matter of feet. I was going so fast that upon hitting the gravel in the gas station lot I spun around three or four times, and barely missed getting hit again by a car pulling out from refueling.

No. 2 – We cut all of the wood which was the only means of heat for the furnace, and we cut all of it ourselves. One time my brother and I were cutting a fairly large tree with a cross-cut saw. Instead of falling straight ahead, the tree twisted to the left and snapped my leg. It was a miracle I wasn't standing further out or it might have been more than just my leg.

No. 3 – Our milk house had a lot of copper, steel and aluminum that was used to separate the milk from the cream. It also had a place to put a cloth to filter out debris. The cream was stored in containers in the deep well until enough was collected to make butter. This particular early fall evening clouds were pitch black. Soon the rain poured and the lightning cracked loudly and often. I could hardly wait to get out of the building which seemed to be a magnet for lightening. The next thing I heard was a loud thunderous boom as I was thrown out of the door and about twenty feet out into the yard. I wasn't hurt but stunned and quickly recovered, running to the cellar where everyone else was waiting for me.

No. 4 – There was a water moccasin that looked like he was peacefully sleeping. Mike said I should pet him. I didn't realize their bite was poisonous and could be fatal, so I reached down to pet this creature. It lunged at me, but my reflexes bound me back faster than his jolt keeping me clear of his attack. Had he been coiled rather than stretched out, I have been told, I would have lost the match.

No. 5 – I had pneumonia five or six times. I believe I caught it from poor nutrition and the fact that I woke up many times during the winter with no blankets or coverings. Mike had them all. As we got older Ma Daly had her own bed in our room. The pneumonia bouts lasted four or five days, sometimes longer. I lost a lot of weight and it took longer each time to get better. The worst was my last round, when walking around like a mummy, I coughed up a large block of green material, which relieved my congestion, allowing me to finally breathe normally. It wasn't long before I headed to the bread box as I hadn't had solid food in quite awhile.

No. 6 – Standing behind the produce truck guiding it back with hand motions in the driver's rear view mirror almost turned fatal. The truck continued back and I was pinned against the cement wall of the building. Although my arm was crushed, had I been over a few more inches, it would have been the end for me. The only reason the driver stopped was he heard the cracking noise from my arm and thought he was running over baskets.

No. 7 – Living in upstate New York after I was married, where we had a lovely home sitting on two acres of mostly wooded property, could have proven to be too much. Our large fireplace could easily contain a person standing up and was about four feet wide. With plenty of wood around our house, I decided to buy a chain saw. Standing on an eight foot ladder, I was cutting a good size limb. The limb snapped and came down smashing the ladder to about three feet. Somehow, I had enough sense to throw the chain saw to

110

the side as I jumped off the dilapidated ladder. I was unscathed and future wood was cut only from smaller trees with my feet planted firmly on the ground.

No. 8 – As I took on more management responsibilities, I relinquished my sales territory little by little so that I could coach and train the new sales representatives. As I trained the new hire, we would ride together. One time, while crossing a two lane bridge from P.E.I. to New Brunswick, a long semi-truck was approaching us in our lane. He must have dozed off but about 200 yards from our car he adjusted back to his lane. It wasn't until after he passed that I had a vision of us being completely demolished as he ran over us.

No. 9 – My wife was pregnant with our second child and I was in Twin Falls, Idaho, at our research farm for the semi-annual review of new crops and varieties for our customers. My sister Marlene, who lived in the west, knew almost by heart, the days in June and August when I would be "out west". She had me paged at the Holiday Inn where I was staying and was so excited when I answered the phone. She couldn't speak fast enough, saying that my brothers Mike and Jack and my other sister Dolly had come out to visit her. She was asking me to spend an extra few days out west to fly in Friday, spend Saturday with them and return home on Sunday. I said I would get right back to her and called my wife to see how she was doing. She said she missed me and was really having a rough time with morning sickness. She went on to say she knew how disappointed I would be but wanted me to come home. I related the phone call to Marlene and took my scheduled trip home. The flight I would have been on to Grand Junction, Colorado from Twin Falls, Idaho, crashed in the Rocky Mountains, killing all 54 on board.

No. 10 – I was fortunate to travel to many countries in my job as Worldwide Sales Manager. I was in the Middle-East interviewing prospective applicants for a sales role, working with the government and distributors. After a few days of interviewing and another week of sales calls I had set-up, it was time to go home. The flight from Damascus, Syria, to London was smooth and uneventful. Thank goodness, we travelled first class when we were abroad. The economy section was first come, first serve, and when at capacity, a company official would shout, "All full! Get back! Sorry! Next plane in two hours or so!" This same plane I was on exploded on the ground the very next day as an onboard passenger lit a Bunsen burner to brew some tea before take-off. This time over one-hundred passengers died.

No. 11 – Even though I was assistant manager after six years, sales were always part of my life. I would occasionally meet the sales people and reinforce our product to customers. After being gone all week, I returned home one Friday. That night we decided to take the kids to a drive-in movie and brought our own drinks and a mammoth bag of popcorn. Part way through the movie, I told my wife Nancy, I wasn't feeling well and it was as though someone had tightened a belt around my waist. The kids were sound asleep, so we left. The next day I felt a little better, but woke up Sunday and called a doctor. He examined me and said it could be a stomach disorder since I did not have a fever and looked normal. After he had gone, I squirmed and moaned for an hour or so, then asked my wife to take me to the hospital. I told three different doctors my symptoms. I gave them my permission to operate, insisting that they do so and once I signed the necessary paperwork, they started preparing me for surgery. The operation went smoothly; they found a ruptured appendix that had formed a pouch at the side of my stomach. Later, when my wife was taken to my recovery room, she was taken to intensive care. I guess this area of the hospital housed everyone just getting out of surgery. She said she heard the heart monitor and started to cry, thinking she was too young to be left alone with three small children. All of the sudden, I was waking up and had these tubes from a machine on my left side going across the bed to my right arm. When she heard me say, "Hey nurse, why in the hell don't you put this apparatus on my right side so I don't get my hands and arms all tangled up." Nancy burst out crying, saying, "Oh honey, that's you alright." I was handed another chance by God who had made plans for me in the future. Another miracle happened that same day. It was July 20, 1969, when Neil Armstrong landed on the moon and said, "One small step for man, one great leap for mankind." When I returned home after a few days in the hospital, the neighbors came by and one by one related how our three year old son Jeff said his daddy was doing okay and the doctor man said he ate so much popcorn and drank so much beer at the movies that he blew his out his stomach.

No. 12 – Nancy and I were driving one Saturday in the fall with our three kids, to visit her grandma, the kid's great-grandma. Before coming to the main road which was Olentangy Boulevard, there was a ravine where a little brook flowed through some fairly large trees. The kids were asleep on each other's shoulders in the backseat and just as I bent forward slightly to adjust the radio, I heard glass shatter and immediately pulled over to the side of the road. The rear window showed a small hole in the center of much broken glass. Luckily, there was a phone booth about a half block away where Nancy called the police. Two officers arrived shortly and after examining the window, said it had been struck by a bullet. The trajectory of the bullet went right behind my head and out the window which was rolled down since it was warm outside and we didn't have air-conditioning. I filled out the necessary paperwork and the policemen told me that perhaps, if I had not bowed slightly to adjust the radio, the bullet could have struck me in the back of my head. The officers took our phone number and address and said they would get back to us. Later that night, the father of the perpetrator called apologizing for his son's actions and said he had confiscated the gun for an indefinite amount of time. He went on to say that we should send all repair bills for the window to him and he would have his son work to pay him back. After this conversation, his son got on the phone and said he was sorry and how foolish he was for shooting at squirrels and birds within the city limits and so close to traffic. He also stated that he was very thankful we were not hurt. Shortly after their call, one of the police officers called to see if the boy had contacted us. He also wanted to know if we wished to press charges. We said that although it was a foolish accident, we heard from the boy and his dad, where they had apologized and said they would make sure all charges for repairs were taken care of, so we did not wish to do so.

No. 13 – Our advertising director Dr. Liddell and I took a helicopter from La Guardia Airport to downtown New York City. All of us on board commented about how noisy and rough the ride was as the helicopter shook like a large tin can swinging in a strong wind.

About two weeks after our voyage, this same helicopter crashed killing eight people.

Boxer, Rocky Graziano said it best in his biography tracking his life as a sad, impoverished child to his eventual triumph as a middleweight champion of the world . . . Somebody up there likes me!

· WILLIAM E · UPJoHN PRIZE ·
AWARDED TO
LYNN A. MILLER
IN RECoGNITIoN oF SPECIAL ACCoMPLISHMENT
THE UPJOHN CoMPANY · 1991

The Upjohn Award: This award was given annually to employees that exhibited outstanding achievment. Only 1 in 1,000 would be accepted and the criteria required to win this coveted award was an awesome challenge. In addition to a generous check, there were salary and stock option increases and an annual gift at Christmas. After being nominated several times ,I finally made it! When I was called announcing my win I hung up the phone and cried with jubilation.

My wife Nancy and I will be married 48 years this August and both share the deep concern for the less fortunate. We have 3 children and 2 grand-children that all love and respect our close knit family. They too give generously of time and money to the church and worthwhile causes. We are so proud of our son and daughter-in-law who work with the church and our grand children who each summer travel with other kids to do chores for the Habitat for Humanity.

Duffer Patrick Miller, what a character! He is much bigger and handsome compared with the first time 10 1/2 years ago when he found us. That scrawny kitten used to chew on plants in the desert to survive and it was no wonder he chewed the blossoms and leaves from a shamrock plant that cost us over $310 in vet bills. He is worth every penny though. This furry alarm clock wakes us each morning with a happy meow to start the day.

Ohio State Univ.
March 1961
2nd Place
Greek Week King

The fraternity brothers caught me in a weak moment and asked if I would represent the frat. house during Greek Week. I agreed and without rehearsal got 4 other brothers to be my backup while I sang Love Letters in the Sand and Catch a Falling Star. After answering a battery of questions , 10 of us finalists were to do a skit for the sororities and girls rooming houses. The next day the votes were tallied and I luckily place 2nd. It wasn!t so much the voice, but the casual and relaxed appearance that did it.

116

From neighbors and fellow workers I collected a record amount that year for the March of Dimes. No Nike shoes or Gatorade then, just Keds and water. I used my feet to lend a helping hand. The walk didn!t seem like the many miles, but the holes in the bottom of my shoes and the soreness of my feet driving home said I did something for a cause and I felt good all over.

The second hand suit with the oil stain on the knee, the home made shirt from a flour or feed sack and the Christmas bow for a tie didn!t bother me. I chose Nicholas for my confirmation name because Nick sounded manly and he was a generous person to the less fortunate...I think I chose a good name. I never considered myself poor, but rich in imagination.

I am standing here with my future mother-in-law who said she was so proud of me .She scolded the foster ladies Loretta and Jane for their treatment of me and absconding with my hard earned money for college. We turned away and went to a nice restaurant where I had a hearty lunch and a glass of wine to celebrate 9 years of work and finally getting my diploma. Two days later I was on a plane starting a career that would last 39 years.

This is my highschool picture right before graduation. The principle of the school called me into her office and staring at me exclaimed, "you are a gifted and bright individual with God given talent, but unless you change your careless and reckless attitude the future will not be very good for you." "You could remain defiant and end up in prison the rest of your life or you could multiply those God given talents to become very successful." I had never fogetten those words and am so thankful every day.

This is Max, the Mean Minorca rooster who would flap his wings, peck at me and use his spurs everytime I would go to the "hin" house or the outhouse.

I had enough of this bully so I soaked some bread crusts in beer and tossed it at him. It wasn!t too long before Max was down on the ground and I cautiously approached him with a broom, put my foot on him, pulled his waddles, swatted him in the rear and told him never to pester me again. From that time on everytime I walked past with the broom, he remained in his place and just let out a little crow.

COLLEGE

Preparing for College Life

A big thank you goes to Baldi Thompson for guiding me through college preparation. Baldi lived in Wellington, Ohio, about ten miles from where I lived. Best of all he was studying to be a veterinarian, was a year ahead of me, and knew college life. I too was planning to study veterinarian medicine. He suggested I purchase the medical insurance the college was offering as full coverage was only $5 per quarter. He told me that there would be an introduction packet sent to me in July. I needed to read all of the information carefully before signing up for the insurance. There was one section that covered answers to commonly asked questions and this part certainly helped me.

Two days before my final day working at Piazza's Produce Farm, I was struggling to lift a trailer tongue with dozens of crates of cabbage as cargo. Owner Dominic was on the trailer seat, and as I strained I felt a pop-pop. Dominic came down to help me unaware of what had happened. It was too late for help as I discovered after he left. I walked to the restroom, felt my groin area, and sure enough, there were two enlargements; one on each side. I had just gotten a double rupture or hernias. So that's what they mean by "busting a gut".

Thankfully, I had an easy work schedule the last days before college. Dominic gave me a ride home my last day, shook my hand, and wished me well. It was suggested that we be on campus about a week before school officially began to get acquainted with the atmosphere of college, find living quarters, buy books, and schedule classes.

In my case there was more to do. I left the foster home ten days ahead to buy clothes, get a job or two, and look for a room or apartment. I remember vividly going down the hill to start the 125 mile hitch-hike to Columbus. There were no good-byes or well wishes from the Daly's, which was normal. Loretta stationed herself on top of the hill where she could shout down at me, "Don't you ever think of coming back or asking for another dime, because you won't get it and mark my words, you will be begging to come back". I didn't say, "Go to hell", in my mind she was already there. I had a meager $300 with me for tuition, books, and living expenses. Growing up, I always had to sign my hard earned checks over to the Daly's, and never once did I see my account balance. I never knew the total of the money I had earned over five years, but my older brother had visited before I left for college to ask if I really wanted to spend my money on school. He said that I was just $400 short of $4,000 which could buy a new Corvette. Although he was shown the checkbook, I never did see it. Who knows what happened to that money after I left, I received very little of it.

A few hundred yards from the Daly encampment was a creek where I had spent many days fishing, swimming, and drinking the cool water from upstream falls. Stopping, I threw my bag of shoddy clothes in the water where it landed with a big splash. After three or four rides, I was in Columbus where I looked up Baldi who said I could spend a couple of days at his fraternity house until I found a place. Freshmen were ineligible to join a fraternity; that would come later.

Monday was spent going to Redwood and Ross men's clothing store with chic apparel for students. I introduced myself to the owner, Marvin, and told him my plight. Bless his heart! After agreeing to let me make payments he helped me pick out an array of "stud" clothes that included black oxford loafers; olive, gray, blue, and tan slacks; and blue, yellow, and white button-down shirts. We were not even half way done when several challis ties, two herringbone sport coats, a London Fog raincoat, several sweaters, a camel hair hat, socks, belts, and underwear were added to the pile. I told Marvin I would never be late in making a payment as I was scheduling at least thirty hours of work per week. He shook my hand, patted me on the back, and told me he trusted me. He also told me that I had an honest looking face. I studied the classifieds in the Columbus Dispatch for a place to stay and found an upstairs room in a home with three other guys. It was located on Chittenden Avenue which was ideal as it was only five blocks from the Student Union. The next several days were spent matching the classes I needed with my intended work schedule. Finally, my time was spent finding work which turned out to be pretty easy and close by. I served up food and washed dishes at the local high school, waited tables at the only Jewish sorority on campus, and always found extra work on weekends or holidays doing painting, landscaping, or other chores. I worked carefully, cleaned up afterwards, and always asked for an inspection of my work. Most of the homes where I worked gave me good tips knowing that I was a college student.

A couple days before school officially opened, I made an appointment for a physical which was mandatory. On my visit, the doctor noticed my hernias, and asked when it happened. I told him two weeks prior lifting weights. Fortunately, I had insurance, and was told I would need a recheck in a couple of weeks. In the meantime, he would set a date for the hernia operation during Christmas vacation. Work alternated with my classes, I met many new friends, and readily adapted to college life. I always had to plan ahead to meet my financial obligations and do well in school. I was told by my doctor that the hernia operation was scheduled for December 28 in Elyria. It was good that I had gotten the early notice so that I could plan to work extra hours to be sure I had a cushion when the high school and sorority were closed for the Christmas holiday. Now I had to figure out where I could go to make the necessary extra dollars. One day, I remembered a high school classmate's dad who was a prominent attorney say, "If I ever needed help, to call him". I dialed John Radican's dad to ask if there was a remote chance that my father had an insurance policy when he died. I related the details I knew about my father's employment at the Thew Shovel in Lorain, Ohio, the St. Joseph church our family had attended, and the hospital where he died. Two days later I got a call saying my father did have a small policy that we were entitled to. I thanked Mr. Radican profusely, calling Mr. Lufton, the contact person I had been given, right away. Mr. Luften told me there was indeed life insurance and each of us was entitled to $350. I gave him my address so that he could send me a check. "Hot damn", I kept repeating over and over to myself. Now I had some funds to carry me over the holidays allowing me to spend a few days recouping from my operation before going back to school or work.

The day before Christmas when campus was empty, I walked downtown looking at the storefront displays and the last minute shoppers who could hardly carry all of their purchases. For lunch, I went to the Seafood Bay Restaurant to have a bowl of lobster bisque and a glass of chardonnay to celebrate my lucky find of the life insurance money. After lunch, several hours passed while I wandered around, stopping but not shopping. It was so nice to see people happy and greeting each other with "Merry Christmas". It would be so good if people greeted each other this warmly all the time. At 5:30 pm it was dark already so I headed back to my room at the fraternity. About two blocks from my college home, I stopped at Ptomaine Tommy's. This place catered to the college kids with great hot dogs, chili dogs, and hamburgers. The sign in the window said, "Seating capacity 1200 - 30 at a time". I scoffed down a bowl of chili blackened with pepper and topped with lots of onions and cheese. Before leaving I ordered two chilidogs to go. As I turned down Chitteden Avenue most of the houses were dark, although there was an occasional glow of multi-colored Christmas lights. It was a quiet and peaceful evening. Since I was quite warm after hoofing it home I decided to sit on the porch swing to enjoy my two chili dogs. As I turned onto the walkway leading to the porch I sensed I was being followed. After stopping I pivoted around to find a beautiful, brown-eyed, bushy-tailed squirrel. I called her Samantha after a squirrel I had met in a city park ten years ago. I sat on the swing and made a "nic, nic, nic" sound, and she came up to join me for Christmas Eve dinner. Samantha sat on her haunches with her paws together reminding me to say prayers before my meal. "Bless this food, my furry guest, and this day. Amen". I had to share the entire chili dog with my Christmas companion as it would not have been fair to her to just give her part of the bun.

I could hardly believe it, but on December 27th a check arrived at the address in Columbus I had given the lawyer. No way was I going to have the check sent to La Grange. Talk about timing! I was happy and relieved and felt good all over. My operation was scheduled for the following day at 10:30 a.m. I hitchhiked to the hospital arriving at 8:30 am to fill out the necessary papers, and read and signed the waivers. I don't remember much until I woke up in the recovery room where I met some very nice, pretty nurses. One nurse in particular named Mary asked if I had urinated yet. I said, "No", and she told me if I did not go within the next four hours, she would have to catheterize me. That made me nervous, so I asked to run some water since that always made me have to go. She smiled at my anxiousness as I started concentrating on my goal . . . go, go, pee, pee. After an hour and a half I was more than happy to show Mary the pint or so of yellow gold.

They only kept me in the hospital for two days before releasing me. I called the Daly's with "Season's Greetings", telling them of my operation. Jane insisted that I come back and rest for a day before going back to campus. It was a mild reception with nothing being asked about my operation or college life. I called a high school friend and he told me there was a party for the kids who were home from school that would be held the next evening. I never hesitated to pick up the phone in college, but this was the first time in eleven years that I had used the phone at the Daly's. I slept in the next day, exchanged niceties, and left at 5 pm, with my belongings in a small duffle bag, to go to the party. It was good to see my high school friends, and I even danced a couple dances although I was stiff and a little sore. I left around 9:30 pm to get a ride back to Columbus. Once there I cashed the $350 check putting $300 in the bank, and taking $50 to enjoy good food, wine, and even a couple of taxi rides. This was a Christmas present to myself. The second quarter of school was a few days away, and I was ready. I recouped rapidly, never missed school, my work, or my payments to Redwood and Ross.

CHANGING MAJORS – A MAJOR DECISION

Ever since I could remember, I wanted to go to college to study to be a veterinarian. My love of animals, and my mentor Dr. Tom, who came out to the Daly farm periodically, kept my ambition alive. I took the necessary classes in pre-vet, but when it came time to enter the veterinary college, I sensed from the prerequisites that I wouldn't be a candidate. If one of my parents or relatives was a vet and attended Ohio State University; that was a plus. Donating to the college was another plus, and understudying with a vet for at least two summers ranked very high. Not meeting any of the criteria, especially the last one, training two summers without pay shut out my life-long ambition.

While looking for other types of educational interests I took a class in fermentation since it involved making wine, sauerkraut, and pickles. My first assignment was to make sauerkraut. Following the directions, I bought six large heads of cabbage, shredded them after quartering, added salt and water, and placed the material in a large crock with a plate and stone over the top and a spigot on the bottom. I was to take a sample every day and measure the PH until it reached the specific level where it should be canned. What a tedious job so I just added some salt every day or two for a few days, then tasted it. It was crunchy and very good. Dr. Gould suggested the class taste my batch, for which they all gave me thumbs up. The very next day I wasn't feeling so great, and called in sick with flu symptoms. My girlfriend, Nancy, brought me various juices telling me to drink plenty of fluids and get rest. After having diarrhea for two days everything seemed normal again. I called Dr. Gould to tell him I would be back to class and work having recovered from a slight bout with the flu. He said, "Flu, hell, you wiped me out and all the other 25 students in class". He took a sample of the sauerkraut to Dr. Weiser, head of the bacteriology department, and it came back loaded with some strain of foreign bacteria, which made everyone sick.

Support bacteria; they're the only culture some people have
– anonymous

After this class, Dr. Gould pulled me aside to say that there are many fields out there to go into, but the 'food' industry is the largest in the world. It offers unlimited opportunities and he wanted me to consider this for my major; which I did.

In our classes, we froze some fruit and vegetables, but mostly canned products. Our lab required us to come in on our spare time to condense tomato juice to a specific viscosity so that we could make and can ketchup. One of the students was a wealthy guy from Egypt named Salah. He said that he would pay me to help him make the ketchup. Since he was paying me by the hour, each time he left the room, I would add more water to the batch. I told Salah I was privy to the wine codes and suggesting that we open a can or two. He said, "Oh no, Dr. Gould would know because that is one product he watches like a hawk". I suggested we empty out two wine cans and two pumpkin cans. We could drink the wine, pour the pumpkin in two new cans, and label them with the wine code. He said, "I must admit you are nothing short of a genius". The extra two hours didn't seem long with us laughing and enjoying our discovery. To my dismay, a few days later, Dr. Gould said, "Let's sample some of the products we processed". Good Lord, this was not good news I thought. The first two cans he opened were tomatoes as labeled. Next was a potato can and a green bean can which also were fine. Just as I thought luck was on my side, he opened a can of wine with pumpkin in it. He immediately said, "Miller, how many cans did you switch?" I shot back, "Why me?" and he said, "You are the only one savvy enough to try to pull such a stunt".

On many occasions, I tried Dr. Gould's patience. One of such 'tests' was when a group of Japanese businessmen came to visit the food lab. I came in early so the lab would pass the white glove inspection since I was told to have the place spotless. Just as I was putting on the finishing touch, Dr. Gould came in from his office, escorting about twenty men. He introduced me as a "bright and promising student", then turned to me in a whisper and said, "How about leaving before you botch something up." While turning to leave, I accidently stepped on the handle of the large hose I had used to wash down the lab. I heard a loud "whew" as the pressure lifted this slight visitor about three inches off the ground. The hose was shooting water all over the place, and the visitors were looking for cover. Grabbing the hose I brought it over to the large cleaning area where I shut off the water. As I left, Dr. Gould and the others were wiping themselves off from all of the water that had sprayed them.

I had quite a few mishaps in the lab, but one was by far the worst. In mid-summer, the horticulture department had picked two flat beds of tomatoes, and had taken notes on fruit per vine, size, variety, weight per plant, and number of tomatoes still on the vine. Early Saturday morning the two loads were parked outside the lab. It was now our turn to do further evaluations. There were PH readings, color, skin thickness, and juice samples. The next steps included washing, peeling, and juice extraction. This took most of the day. About 5 pm, Dr. Gould said, "Boys, you all worked very hard today, and I am very proud of you. We should be done in an hour, so as a reward I am ordering pizza for all of us". Then the shock of my life came, "Miller, you are in charge of the filler and canning operation". I wanted to say something, but he left, and I was in charge. Having never been mechanically inclined, you can imagine how uptight I was at all of these gauges, clanging of cans, steam pouring out, spigots, and chain links with cans on them slowly going by. "Holy tomato", after about a half hour I looked at the cans at the other end, and they were empty. I said to myself, "I know, I'll bet the stainless steel holding tanks got backed up and the vacuum took the juice to another tank". Wrong! In a panic I went to the area where the "filled" cans were supposed to be. Lifting each can one by one I found we only had a single can of juice. At that moment Dr. Gould came out, clapped his hands and said, "Well, Mr. Miller how did we do?" I told him we only got one can. He said, "You mean one case", and I repeated, "One can". Carefully, he went to each piece of equipment finding that whoever had previously cleaned the holding vats had not closed the valves at the bottom. As the juice was coming over, it was going down the drain. It seemed so simple to find the problem when he did it. Dr. Gould's assistant, Dr. Geisman and post graduate student, Winston Bash, could hardly control themselves with this last antic of mine. They were both in the hall doubled up when Dr. Gould said to me, "You know what very dumb is, well, you are even dumber than that"!

Even with this declaration, he had a heart of gold. On a couple of Saturdays when I worked to make extra money, he would come by the lab to see me. He would often say, "Here's a ticket to the game now get out of here". He told me he would do the work and record the hours for me. One time he told me, "I like you. You sometimes challenge my patience, in fact, most of the time".

Later we got a large amount of money from the National Potato Institute to do research on varieties for chips as well as other products like fries or potato puffs. I was invited with Dr. Gould and Dr. Geisman to go to a convention and present some of our results. The meeting and presentations went very well as we got great accolades. After dinner, on the way back to school Dr. Gould bought each of us an expensive cigar. I believe it was a Bering that came in a silver colored aluminum tube. Inside the cigar was wrapped in a cedar sheath. The two doctors were in front, and I was in the back seat. All of a sudden, Dr. Gould started coughing and gagging, and he looked in the rear view mirror, and said, "No wonder it stinks in here. You are supposed to take the cedar wrapper off before you smoke the cigar". How would I know? This was my first real quality cigar. This I know, since we were told they cost around $6 apiece when he handed them out.

Two of my last reports I wrote must have impressed Dr. Gould. A couple of weeks before graduation, he asked if I would consider going for my master's and doctorate degrees on an all expense paid scholarship. Before I could answer, he said, "Although you could probably screw up corn flakes for breakfast, you have a certain charisma that the staff and students are drawn to". This was witnessed by the increasing enrollment into food technology along with classes that were fun to say the least. I respectfully declined saying I really wanted to get out into the world after nine years of working and studying. He paused telling me that he certainly understood, but if I ever needed help or changed my mind, to let him know. He closed with, "I must say, Lynn, you certainly brought some welcomed life into our lab".

While interviewing with various companies, they often would ask for a recommendation and I always listed Dr. Gould with his permission, of course. An absolute glowing report was given as read back to me in part, a few years later from one of the Senior Vice Presidents of Asgrow, David F. Behrent.

I wasn't privy to all the information Dr. Gould wrote, but after working for Asgrow for a couple of years, Dave had to relate some comments from Dr. Gould. Here is a portion of what he wrote: Each time, and there were many, I admonished or demeaned Lynn for the really 'unique' things he did in the lab, he always said in a sheepish way, "I know", and never ever argued. Later at a dinner with neighbors or at a staff function, I would relay the experiences and the whole group would be breaking up with laughter. Lynn was a serious challenge, but a pleasure because he was a magnet that drew other students to the class and eventually a major. Our 300% gain in students majoring in food technology was due in no small part to this wonderful character who fortunately came my way and made the class and my work fun, exciting, and full of surprises. I envy the company that lands this prize. Dr. W. A. Gould

R.O.T.C. – MARCHING, SHOOTING A HOLE IN THE ROOF, AND AN AWARD

The initials R.O.T.C. stood for Reserve Officers' Training Corp and it was a mandatory class for two years at Ohio State University. If there ever was a class I despised, this was it. The instructors were arrogant, gung-ho, loud, and acted as though the military was the best profession next to being the Pope. I selected the Army rather than the Navy or Air Force for no particular reason. Class was two hours once a week, and we had to put on brown uniforms, shine the brass buttons on our coats, and spit polish our shoes. The first quarter was devoted to listening to war stories, heroes, and how we beat our enemy with surprise attacks and superior weaponry. I must say this was the best of the two year program. The second quarter was a disaster because I hated the marching drills we went through as the drill instructor would bark out the commands. We would march 1, 2, 3, 4; and then some shouting of 'about face'. A couple times I almost wiped out the whole platoon as I got messed up in the "about face" deal. The drill instructor said he was reporting me for not being cooperative, causing low morale, and even talking and laughing during drills. I knew I would get called on the carpet, but one of my misfortunes again came to my rescue. In a subtle voice, I told Captain Fenner that I had a hernia operation during the Christmas break, and it was very awkward to turn on a dime. The 'about face' was cumbersome for me as I hurt while we marched. He said if I got a report from my doctor, it would not be necessary for me to march or take place in any of the drills. I submitted the doctor's report, and Captain Fenner asked me if I could type. I told him no, in fact, I had never even used a typewriter. He scratched his head, then said I could perform some jobs around like washing windows, cleaning the restroom, and sweeping floors.

My roommate, Jack Swigert, was really gung-ho Army R.O.T.C. the same branch I was in. Of course, he wasn't working his way through school like me, so he would come from the fraternity house right before R.O.T.C. and put on his neatly pressed pants and shirt, spit shined shoes, and his coat with brilliantly shined brass buttons. One day, as a joke, I inserted 'General Electric' on top of his name on his tag. Jack must have been in a hurry that particular day because he never even noticed and the whole platoon could hear him get cussed out for a joke that was not funny to him.

It was in early December during finals that I told Jack, who had just come back from studying at the library, that Captain Fenner called and was having just a select few for a Christmas party. He was asking each person to bring a dish to pass, and wanted Jack to bring some chocolate chip cookies for the event. I told Jack to call Captain Fenner around 11 p.m. when the captain would be returning from a late dinner. "Hello, Captain Fenner, this is Jack Swigert, I can surely bring some chocolate chip cookies to the party". Then I could hear, "Oh, I am so sorry about the late call . . . I must have gotten the wrong message". We all got the biggest laugh out of this; even Jack had to say it was funny a bit later.

I never did like guns, fully put together, or disassembled so that we could put it together blindfolded. I felt uncomfortable handling any weapon. Unfortunately, the last semester was all about guns. Our instructor told us to load our gun with live ammunition, making sure the barrel was always pointed up to avoid accidently pulling the trigger. Somehow, I managed to squeeze the trigger on this object that I hated even while I held it as I had been directed. The whole class heard the gun go off and was in awe. Captain Fenner came over to me, grabbed the gun out of my hand, and said he would deal with me later. For now I needed to get out of the building. He was still grousing at me as I left, adding that I should be prepared to be expelled from school for shooting a hole in the ceiling. This was not a good day as it was the same day I had dropped out of chemistry because I could not understand the professor's Russian accent, the fraternity was going to kick me out for bringing beer into the house, and now this, a threat to be kicked out of school. Plan B was to call the Marines since I would be out of school and I could apparently use their discipline. I tried to call three times, but each time I called the phone rang busy. This must have been God's plan. This plan also told me to stick it out by trying to stay in school. I decided the next day to go to the armory on my way to the high school where I worked washing dishes to apologize and plead my case. I asked one of the gentlemen in the armory where I might find Captain Fenner. He told me he was probably in the lunch room since it was right around noon. I ran up the stairs, swung open the lunch room door, and what did I see but a poker game going on with real money on the table. I was told to get out, but I went in, and said to Captain Fenner that I would like to see him for just a minute. He came out shortly, somewhat red faced, and said it was only a fun game, and that they did not always play for money. I charged right back saying that I saw nothing, and that I wanted to be reinstated in R.O.T.C., not reported, or expelled. I extended my hand, he shook it firmly, saying that I had potential as a leader, but I needed to be careful when ammunition was involved.

The semester before I got a C- in R.O.T.C. primarily because I couldn't fold a large unfolded military map blindfolded. I had a difficult time with my eyes wide open, and I could not put a gun together either. My logic, which the instructor did not appreciate, was to just suppose the enemy comes up to me in a surprise attack . . . does one say, "Hold it right there, you dirty enemy – I have to put this gun together, and don't you think they could hear you folding a map?" Crunch, crunch, crunch!

After I got reinstalled, we all had our turn at target practice. We wheeled cardboard targets about 100 feet away and started shooting. We were taught the basics on aiming, and we could wheel our targets in to examine our hits or misses. For an exam, we were to come in on our own, go to the desk upstairs, and get 15 shells. Five of these were for practice, and the remaining ten were to be fired at the target which was then handed in. I only hit the target in one place in practice, and it was near the top left hand corner. I wheeled the target in, and the hole that the bullet made was about the size of a small pencil. With the practice target, I jabbed quickly with a pencil and made it look like I shot some amazing shots. I got the new unblemished target, matched it up with the practice target and punched the holes. Of course, I had broken off the lead and just "shot" all over the place. I fired off ten rounds so the person at the desk could hear me. Fortunately, it must have been near lunch because no one else was around to witness my feat. I turned the target in, and the person at the desk looked at it and said what a good shot I was. A week later in our last class I was asked to stand up and be acknowledged for shooting an amazing 94%, the second best of 1500 or so. Everyone applauded and later shook my hand. Captain Fenner said he would like me to consider joining the elite Pershing Rifles, but I said I respectfully had to decline because of my school and work schedule.

Finding a Lost Sister

My sister, Marlene, was living in Grand Junction with her husband Frank who was the District Attorney. I took a train called the California Zephyr to visit her and had been awake most of the trip with a group of college kids who got on in Chicago. Once arriving at Marlene's house I think I slept most of the afternoon, got up for dinner, and then went back to sleep. A few days after my arrival, they told me we were going to Aspen, Colorado with a group of lawyer friends. We had tickets to see the Smothers Brothers at the Purple Onion. I believe it was one of their first times on stage, and a couple of the guys in our group were asked to leave when they kept shouting, "Who's the mother of the Smothers Brothers?"

After a couple of Moscow Mules, the popular drink made up of ginger beer, vodka, and lime juice, my sister leaned over saying that it was a shame I had never met Karen. I asked, "Who is Karen?" She said, "Our youngest sister who was adopted not long after being born". Frank overheard the conversation and told her to be quiet, but she insisted on talking about Karen so I listened. When I got back to school, I contacted my high school friend, John Radican, and asked to speak to his dad who was the lawyer who had told me, "If you ever need anything, just let me know". I told him the story of my adopted sister; that we lived in Lorain, Ohio at the time, and gave him other particulars to use. Two days later, Mr. Radican called to say that our sister Karen was adopted by the Morrison's who lived in Berea, Ohio. On Friday, I took a bus to Berea, and then took a cab to the address I was given. The people that answered the door could not help me with my inquiry so I went down the street ringing doorbells till I found a family who said they remembered a couple that brought home a baby with red hair 18 to 20 years before. They remembered they had moved so I got a phone book and located the Morrison's. I went to the house, knocked on the door, and when I said I was Karen's brother, Mrs. Morrison tried to shut the door in my face, but I had my foot against it. After forcing my way in and asking politely to see Karen, she said, "Karen is not here". I then asked if I could see her room. When I opened the closet there was only one sweater there. I also got a glimpse of a picture of her in that room. I told Mrs. Morrison that I was almost twenty years old so Karen had to be nineteen, and with an empty closet, she had to be away at college. Mrs. Morrison said, "Yes, but I will not tell you where". Now I was getting upset, so I fired back, "I intend to have my whole college fraternity take turns calling different colleges starting in Ohio, and then spilling this story to Karen once I find her". I had called her bluff because she said, "Okay, she is at Ohio State". That was amazing since that is where I was too. She asked me to introduce myself as a cousin because they had relatives named Miller. She went on to say if I cooperated, they would tell her the truth after a year was up. This was very difficult for them since they had never told Karen that she was adopted. After a few days, I called Karen, and said I would like to meet her, but after being told that I was a distant cousin, there was no rush to get together. I set up a meeting for a week later, and when I got to her dorm, her "parents" were there which caused our meeting to be casual and cool.

When the year was up, I called the Morrison's to remind them of the deadline. Mr. Morrison shouted over the phone that if I dared to tell the real story, he would sue me for every dime I had. I laughed and said, "I will send you a check now for 75 cents". Years later, I engaged my brother-in-law, the District Attorney from Grand Junction, who said he would trace Karen who was now out of college and married. He located Karen, and all of us, two sisters and three brothers broke the news to her and her husband. She took the information we shared with her very poorly, and said, "That's nice, but I don't want to see you again because my adoptive parents showed me so much love and attention ". That was the end of our meeting with our lost sister who had rejected all she had to gain from the family she had never met before.

SPRING BREAK

During spring break one year, my sister, Marlene, sent me a train ticket to visit her and husband, Frank, in Grand Junction, Colorado. The train left Columbus in the late afternoon, and arrived in Chicago around 11 pm departing the next morning at 4 am I really didn't have a lot of extra money for a hotel, and anyhow, I might have overslept or not slept at all constantly looking at the clock. There was a bar not too far from the train station so I decided to have a glass of wine or two and a sandwich to kill time. As I was eating, in struts something with heavy make-up, wire-brush hair, red high heels, and a furry stole. She plunked herself down next to me, slings the stole around my neck, and said, "Honey, you are my man tonight so how about buying me a drink to get started?" I didn't say yes, but the bartender poured her a glass of champagne and placed the bill in front of me. I tried to look at the damage inconspicuously with my one eye as she was tugging the stole even tighter around my neck. Holy Toledo! I saw the bill was $11 just for that one glass. I had to get out of there before she had a couple more or chocked me to death. She could have easily depleted all the extra cash I had for my trip. Acting very calmly, I waited a few minutes as she was gulping down her first drink, and told the bartender to give us one more. Now she was smiling and slobbering on my cheek. I unwrapped this fox or possum thing around my neck and excused myself to go to the bathroom. Just as I hoped, the bathroom had a window that I could reach if I stood on the toilet seat. I carefully lifted the latch on both sides, rolled the window out, and jumped for about a four foot drop. I ran and ran thankful that I had said nothing about the train I was going to catch. I could imagine some thugs coming at me, beating me to a pulp.

THE TRIALS AND REWARDS IN FRATERNITY LIFE

Now that I was a full-fledged active member in the fraternity, I was voted to be social chairman in charge of parties, dances, and fund raisers. We badly needed and wanted a good stereo, but the price tag for a good one like a Fisher was around $650. At one of our meetings, someone suggested selling popcorn as a fund raiser, but this was rejected because we did not have a vendor's license. The next suggestion was to have a dinner for a sorority and charge them. This was also rejected by all thinking it was a very dumb idea. I came up with the solution saying that we were up to 30 members from 7, and if we really went all out, we could get 30 more for a total of 60. With that count, we could bill each member a little more than $10 and have the better of two worlds . . . the members we needed and the stereo. The idea passed, and our goals were met.

Before the vote to kick me out of the fraternity for bringing in beer, I asked if I could say a few words since I was representing myself. There was a rule that no one was allowed to bring alcoholic beverages into the fraternity house. At first, I thought of my access to two lawyers – roommate Jeff's dad and Mr. Radican who had said to call him anytime. After thinking it over, I felt I could win this case without outside help.

The fact was I didn't bring beer in; I hoisted it up in a leather book bag. The bag held eight beers, and I found a rope in the basement that I tied around the bag, and then threw the rope up to the second floor window. Now I was not walking in with beer, just pulling it up after going inside and opening the window. Someone on the first floor must have seen the rope and cargo go by and reported it. Another member saw me carry the bag to my room. Although I shared the beer with two other members, I was not about to squeal on them.

I calmly got in front of the members and said, "I would like to see a show of hands on how many have ever brought in alcoholic beverages to these premises or ever participated in drinking some". At first there was one hand raised, then three more, now ten, and the last count was almost twenty. I suggested the case be thrown out, and as social chairman I would petition the college to allow alcoholic beverages in the fraternity. It took a while, but eventually permission was given – a victory for me!

One evening after returning from my job of serving dinner to about three dozen sorority girls, I was asked to a special meeting at the fraternity. The basis was to ask me to run for Greek Week King. Heck, all I had to do was sing, smile at the gals, and hope to get their votes. I was in a good mood, and not even thinking of the ramifications as I said, "Sure, why not?"

There were quite a few guys from all the fraternities that decided to run assembled in front of a panel of girls who asked each of us questions pertaining to college life. I rattled off my work schedule, my change in majors, and some of the challenges I met in the fraternity, such as, getting a full membership, buying the stereo, soliciting a plea and getting beer allowed in fraternity houses. Out of the group, ten were selected of which I was one. We were to have a three foot by three foot picture made and placed on a sorority lawn. My fiancé, Nancy, was an Alpha Phi so I got my face on their lawn. The next thing the contestants had to do was ride in a convertible around the oval with the homecoming queen and her court. Each of us had a pretty girl at his side, and we waved at the students along the way. Now before the final vote, we had to go to all the sororities and perform for the gals. I did not have the faintest idea what I was going to do. The day before the travelling show I decided to sing. I picked four, good-looking guys from the fraternity, and told them we should all dress alike, and they could be in the background singing. We were pretty sharp with our blue blazers, blue buttoned-down shirts, no tie, and grey slacks. I decided to sing Perry Como's "Catch a Falling Star" and Pat Boone's "Love Letters in the Sand". A few days later, I got a call from the voting committee saying I was the runner-up. Just think about it, me the runner-up in the Greek Week festival. I was even honored with a trophy! The trophy stayed on the mantle of the fraternity house, although my recent inquiry about it revealed that it could not be located. After scouring through past photos, my wife found the picture of me with my trophy.

GRADUATION

Spring flew by, and before I knew it, graduation was at hand. Guess who showed up? Loretta and Jane!!! They were going to promote the fact that one of the 43 urchins they raised made it through college. I sat with the other agriculture students, and when my name was called, I accepted my diploma, walked across the stage, stopped, bowed, and waved to my fiancé and her parents. It was a long, long journey, but I made it just like I knew I would in the orphanage when I accepted my first academic award 15 years earlier. Nancy gave me a big hug, and said she was so proud of me, and her parents patted me on the back, telling me, "Good job". Jane and Loretta started walking my way, but I turned the other way to exit the auditorium. Sylvia, always full of spunk, turned and said to them, "We are taking him to a very nice restaurant, and we are going to buy him a celebration drink and dinner, and by the way, you are not welcome".

The following day, while clearing out my room at the fraternity, I looked at a piece of paper I kept on my desk with the words, "Dreams are free; college is a little more expensive". I felt like a tremendous burden had been lifted off my shoulders!

Accept the challenges so you may feel the exhilaration of victory
– General George S. Patton Jr.

MARRIAGE AND FAMILY

DATING AND MARRYING NANCY

Nancy came from a modest family living in a two bedroom, one bath home with a long driveway and an unattached garage. This home on the north side of Columbus was purchased in 1940 for $4,100. Her dad, Norman, and Uncle Clarence had a small shoe pattern manufacturing company that employed Nancy's two cousins, Jack and Jerry, and a few other people. This business not only supported her parents, but also her grandma, Uncle Clarence and Aunt Lillian, and Aunt Bernice and her family which included seven children. As more and more shoes were produced overseas, a need for this specialty dried up. While I was in college and dating Nancy I did have many excellent meals at that house. La Mere (French name that I used for Nancy's mom) would never ask for money from me directly, she would rather have it in labor. She loved gardening and knew that I did too. One day we were both standing in the front of the house when she said, "Do you suppose we could build a sandstone wall to contain some flowers and shrubs?" Well, I did it. Another time a small piece of wallpaper was hanging down, and she reached up, yanked it down, and said, "Oh dear, look what I have done". It would not have been so bad taking the paper off the ceiling and walls if it wasn't underneath about seven coats of paint, one of which was oil-based. We scored the walls and ceiling then rented a steamer to remove the paper. It was a hot and messy job anyway but in Mid-September with the outside temperatures being warm, it was multiplied inside. Nancy's dad came home from work, took one look, turned around, and left for a couple hours. It was several weeks before we got all the paper off and repainted, but La Mere was delighted with my efforts.

There was another project a few weeks later. Their long blacktop driveway was crumbling, had some large pot holes, and was very uneven. La Mere bought several five gallon pails of black top dressing to fix up the driveway. I told her that I did not think this was the right stuff, but she insisted because it said for use on driveways. This was dressing for a thin coat, not filling in pot holes or leveling. The instructions said to apply it then let it dry for 24-36 hours. We filled the holes and cracks, waited the appropriate amount of time, and took down the barricades. La Mere pulled her car onto the driveway and headed for the garage. Squish, squish, splash, squish, splat. Those pot holes were too deep to dry in such a short time, if they would have dried at all. The car tires picked up quite a bit of tar from the dressing, and were now the size of truck tires. All she could say was, "Oh shoot, I don't think this was a good idea". We had to take our shoes off before coming into the house or we would have had a room full of black tracks. This project wasn't as successful as the others.

We told Nancy's parents we were planning to get married on Saturday, August 19, 1961, a little over two months after I graduated. Her dad, who was an avid golfer, said, "Thanks a lot; that is the date of our country club's invitational". I left for training in Idaho where Asgrow grew crops and harvested them in a place the plant breeders called home. I faithfully sent my pay checks home to Nancy where she was busy getting an apartment for us and furnishing it. The apartment she rented on the second floor, was small, but adequate with a living room-dining room combination, kitchen, one bedroom, and a bath. The $91/month included utilities, and other than the $189 for a bedroom set, the rest of the apartment Nancy furnished with used furniture at the cost of about $100. She purchased a refrigerator for $15, a sofa for $10, glass coffee and end tables for $15, and a card table and four chairs for $20. The little bit of money left over was used for kitchen utensils. I returned to Ohio one week before the wedding. Nancy and her mom saw examples of wedding dresses in various showrooms, but they were too expensive so they bought the material and sewed her wedding dress.

Other than a few family members, there were 20 or so fraternity brothers at the wedding. After the ceremony, we headed to Lincoln Lodge where we had the reception. The weather was not too hot, and perfect for an outdoor celebration that included punch and cake, along with candies, mints and nuts. I insisted on chocolate cake although most wedding cakes at the time were made of white cake. After greeting the guests and taking pictures, my fraternity brothers decided to toss me in the pool. My sister, Marlene, pleaded for them not to do this, but they just laughed and did it all the same. Some of the people in the pool got out, but a few clung to the sides getting a big kick out of me doing the dog paddle across the pool in my tuxedo.

On the way back to our apartment, it was even funnier to see the people on the street or in their cars looking at us. Here I was sitting in the front seat by our best man, and Nancy was in the back seat with our maid-of-honor while the sign on the back of the car read "Just Married". Nancy did not want me to sit next to her and get her wedding dress all wet. I asked my brother later what the tuxedo shop thought of the damp outfit. He had told them it was very hot in church because the air conditioner was broken, and the groom was very nervous.

My Wife was an Angel to Her Students

Nancy went four semesters in a row her last year of college. She had several scholarships and graduated when she was just 20 years old with a degree in secondary education in biology and health. At first she was somewhat apprehensive teaching the poorer and underprivileged kids as witnessed by the individual reports on each. Most were from broken homes where the parents were divorced or incarcerated. As the days and weeks passed, she grew to like the students, and they appreciated her concern for each of them. Once we had the whole homeroom class over to our apartment courtyard where we played music, provided soft drinks and snacks, and gave them an opportunity to dance and enjoy themselves. We chaperoned a few school dances and danced right along with the kids. They thought we were really cool, and even told their teacher Nancy that I was very nice.

One program the school had was to show off the student's athletic abilities. The one for basketball had the boys form two lines where a student would dribble the ball and then pass the ball to one student from the other line who was running to catch it and make a basket. The timing was a little off, and the first two collided and fell to the floor. They were not hurt, but this created quite a stir, especially within me. I could not hold back and burst out laughing. Pretty soon the kids and the whole audience were doubling up laughing so hard. Another time, the gym was full to witness a Christmas play put on by the students. After some of the students sung Christmas carols, it was time for Mary and Joseph to enter on their way to Bethlehem. In came this large cardboard donkey, with Mary walking on the back side of it. With the lights dimmed, it seemed as if she were riding it. Joseph had the donkey by a leash leading it very carefully. There was a large silver star in the sky, and Joseph looked up and said, "Hark, man am I getting thirsty". Obviously, he had forgotten his lines, and with those words, I had to explode with laughter as did the rest of the crowd.

It was an educational experience for me, watching Nancy interact with these middle school students. I knew then that she would provide a good home to our future children – a home filled with laughter and love. Nancy retired from teaching after she became pregnant with our first child. From the reaction of her pupils, they may have forgotten some of her lessons, but they probably will never forget how important she made them feel. Each one was special to her, and she found something good in all of them.

FORGIVING MY BROTHER

Nancy and I were in our first home less than a year when I got an urgent call from my brother Mike saying he needed to see me. I was not even aware that he had enrolled at Ohio State University at the suggestion of his fiancé. I rushed to the apartment where he was living, and when he opened the door, I could see right away that something serious was wrong as he was crying incessantly. I started asking questions as he was too upset to talk. "Is your fiancé pregnant?" He shook his head no. Then I told him I could not help him if I don't know the problem. He finally blurted out that he was over $8000 in debt, and the creditors were constantly hounding him. I am positive not too many brothers would come to the rescue of a brother that did the types of things Mike did to me while we were growing up. He spit in my face, urinated on me while I was asleep, pulled covers off me in the wintertime while I slept, perhaps causing my four bouts of pneumonia. He watered down the hundreds of worms I had picked from the grass in the evening that I sold to neighbors. He scalded me with water from the stove as I was bathing, let my champion steer out to get bloated, and laughed when he tipped me off a raft knowing that I could not swim. He and Loretta would have made a great tag team! Mike would gloat seeing me get shocked from a socket that he told me to clean out with a wet rag. He also shot me several times in the buttocks with a BB gun.

None of these things even entered my mind; he was my brother who was a slow learner, wore thick glasses, had irregular teeth, and was not as popular as me. I told him that I would go home, make out a plan, and get back to him in the morning. It was a blessing the company gave me only a few customers at first. I was still busy reading manuals, procedures, results from our many experimental stations, as well as learning the products we sold. When I told Nancy of Mike's situation, she said he could stay with us until he got his finances fixed. We had our two daughters at the time, and we arranged a bed in the same room as Jennifer who was still in a crib. I called Mike the next morning to tell him I would pay his landlord the money due, and that he was most welcome to stay with us until he was debt free. He sighed with relief and told me he would soon be over to move in. All day I went over the plan with him that had kept me awake most of the night. This is the plan that I outlined:

1. Get out of college! You cannot afford it at this time, and your studies would suffer with this cloud over your head. Do not, and I repeat, do not be ashamed of not having a college education because God gave you a different set of talents.

2. Use the talents and experience you have. You have worked for a carpenter, a plasterer, brick layer, and remodeled basements and recreation rooms.

3. Today, let's get some business cards printed L & M (Lynn and Mike) decorating service, and start canvassing the upper Eastside of Columbus where the wealthy people live.

4. Our sales pitch would be that we are paying for college tuition and do almost anything – shampoo carpets, paint, landscape, wash windows, and limited remodeling.

This was a Friday so we set out to get some business cards in color. The card was set in a multi-colored circle with our talents listed boldly. Saturday, we split up to do our canvassing, and were to meet for coffee a few hours later to compare notes. At our first break, I had garnered $1,800 worth of commitments, and Mike bombed out. Mike was floored as I went over our sales pitch again. It helped because at our final get together, the score was $2,700 to $800. This was just our first day, in fact, our first six hours. Now it was to the store to purchase our supplies. Mike said he was a contractor and wanted the applicable discount, which he got. We did not want to get bookings too far in advance because we could clearly see we were onto something to get Mike out of debt. We did our work carefully, always cleaned up after a job, asked for an inspection by the owner, and most of the time got extra work and many referrals. After a few weeks, we were getting quite professional in our pitch such as, "Mam, this area we measured is 12' x 20' or 240 square feet. To shampoo the carpeting, will be $80, and to paint the walls and ceiling will be $150. Of course, we will paint first, and cover the carpeting so as to not get paint on it." We would do the job in one day, and when the customer said how pleased she was, we knew she would tell others.

The debt was dwindling rapidly, and in a little over a year, Mike was debt free and ready to move back to Cleveland to be near his fiancé. He told me later she had told him not to come back till he had all his debts settled. Even though we had given him $400 from our Christmas Club, bought the materials for the first jobs, and let him stay with us for 13 ½ months, he never offered to pay us back. A few days before he left, I suggested he not attempt going to college again; instead use his talents and gifts to go into real estate. I said, "Mike, can you imagine telling a potential buyer that the cabinets are oak, the walls are plaster; not dry wall, and if you want someday to finish the basement, it will cost 'x' dollars, and a multitude of other details". Mike took my advice, and after a couple of years, he was so successful in the Shaker Heights area of Cleveland, the he started his own real estate company. Soon he was making a six figure salary, and he started to become more charitable himself. Eventually, he married and had two children. He finally was using these latent gifts and talents that were awakened when he had bounced back from hitting bottom.

"If we forget about getting revenge and carrying around hate, we will establish peace within ourselves and not suffer the mental state inflicted upon ourselves by seeking revenge and hate".
– Lewis Smedes

A Surprise Birthday Party

While growing up, my subconscious would light a birthday candle for me. It was not until I met Nancy that I talked about how many years it was before I knew my real birthday, and never having any presents or cards.

It was Saturday, November 14, 1965, Ohio State was playing Northwestern, and my wife insisted that I go to the game. She gave her ticket to one of our friends, Tom Brant. We each had a Coke and a hot dog at half time, and after the game, Tom said, "Let's go shoot some pool". I fired back, "No way, Nancy has been with our two girls all day, and I better get home". He made a phone call to Nancy and told me that she wanted me to treat myself and celebrate. Pool was fine, but she reminded me the neighbors had invited us to dinner. After Tom dropped me off, I told Nancy what a great day I had and couldn't wait to go to the neighbors who were capping it off with dinner. After feeding Laura and Jennifer, we read to them and they dozed off as the babysitter arrived. We arrived on time and Pat said it would be about fifteen more minutes because the meal wasn't quite done. Ozzie piped up, "Hey, Lynn and Nancy, let me show you the new terrazzo flooring I put in our recreation room". We went downstairs, opened the door, and when he turned on the lights about thirty guests started singing "Happy Birthday". WOW! It was not a dinner, but a special surprise party that Nancy had organized for my birthday! Friends, neighbors, fraternity brothers, and Nancy's parents were all in on the secret, and did a marvelous job of hiding their cars a block or more away.

I was startled and taken aback. In 25 years, it was the first birthday party that I ever had, and is something I will never forget. We all laughed, joked, and played Charades. We played the guys against the gals. One of the funniest moments of the evening was watching my mother-in-law act out the word stripper. I really think the gals were laughing so hard at her antics that they took their time guessing so that she would continue. Although this was 45 years ago, I think of this party each fall – November 14th that is!

I see God Right There

My dear wife, Nancy, would often read books to the kids, which was quite a feat since we recently added another member to the family, our son Jeff. She often would read religious books depicting, Jesus, Mary, Joseph, and other people from the Bible. One Sunday at church, Jennifer turned and stood up in the pew, saying in a loud voice, "There He is, I see God". We turned her around, but she insisted, tugging at my coat, saying, "Look, daddy, there's God like I told you". We decided to look as Jennifer's eyes were wide. Now she pointed, and said even louder, "There's God". We did have to chuckle as did quite a few parishioners in this little church. There was a man with a long brown beard with his hands folded, eyes shut, softly praying. A few weeks later, our church had a new member in the choir who was singing a beautiful solo. Again this must have impressed Jennifer because she whispered to me, "Daddy I can pray better when the lady is 'songing'".

Some Women Had an Eye for Me

My wife would get the biggest kick out of this woman about 80 years old who would usually position herself either directly in front of or behind us in church. When it came time for the peace offering to each other, she would give me a big smile and a wink. I was always nice to her and would say something like, "Have a wonderful week or God bless you".

EASTER SUNDAY

What a beautiful Easter Sunday in Columbus, Ohio. The forsythia, daffodils, crocus, and tulips were blooming everywhere. Robins were flitting about with straw or grass or anything soft for their nest building, and it seemed as if the whole earth was awakening. I even put lint from the dryer out by the tree so they could pad their nests.

Laura and Jennifer's grandmother made them the prettiest pale yellow floral dresses. We, or I should say, Nancy, found some white bonnets and gloves, patent leather shoes, and white drawstring purses. The girls were three and four years old, and the pride of our lives. We were so excited taking pictures of them on their grandparent's front lawn and then going to church to show off the girls. Once we sat down, not even ten minutes went by before they started swinging their purses at each other. One would wind up and let go, and then the other did the same. Our little pride and joys were quickly turning into our little rascals. I separated them, and scolded them for fighting in church, but that still did not quiet the snickers we heard from the parishioners behind us. They could not get over these two little cuties all dressed up and going at it on Easter Sunday.

Our Move to Upstate New York – Nothing But a Bump in the Road

We moved to New York from Ohio as my territory and responsibilities expanded. My mother-in-law, Sylvia, or as I called her "La Mere", came to visit us and the grandchildren soon after we moved in. She had not been there long when in one day the pipe under the sink burst, the washing machine stopped, and the dishwasher would not work. La Mere started crying, and as she looked at me she asked, "What on earth are you going to do?" I told her we would make a few calls and get everything fixed; that this was part of the cost of moving. While I waited for the respective repairmen, I sent the gals to Heveron's to pick up their great fish dinners which included large portions of Walleye, fries, and coleslaw to bring home along with some nice cold beer. We had dinner, got everything fixed, and went to bed dreaming of better tomorrows.

The very next day while were all together, we decided to listen to some relaxing music from our stereo. Upon turning it on, we didn't hear even a remote sound. Once again, we called an electrician who arrived shortly thereafter. He looked at the stereo, looked around the room, walked to the other side, and flipped on a switch; immediately the music came on. Later we received a bill for $75. I called right away saying even successful corporate lawyers did not make $75 for three minutes work. That equated to $1500 per hour and this was 1966. They finally agreed and settled for $10.

God Handed Us Five to Sponsor and Guide

I said many times later that God had a plan for our move to upstate New York to the small town of East Pembroke. It was there that a neighbor with five children was left on her own as her husband took up with another woman. That 'other' woman just happened to be an attractive Spanish nun who came to town once a week to teach the Catholic children in town their catechism. Our neighbor's husband, Fred, had a roving eye, and soon insisted on taking the kids to class and stayed to drive them home.

The way that we learned about the "affair" happened one day when I was planting some red geraniums and white petunias around the church sign that announced the services and other church events. Father Norman Wheeler who was pastor of the Holy Name of Mary Catholic Church in East Pembroke came out of the church and said how nice my plantings looked. When I was almost finished, the church janitor, Kelton, who also cleaned some other buildings around town, whispered, "Last night when I went to the broom closet, I found Fred and Sister Carmelita in a passionate clench in there. Fred shut the door and said, "For God's sake, can't we have any privacy here!"

Our neighbor Pat, worked as a guidance counselor at a high school in Clarence, a town about 20 miles from us. Since she was not at home when the children got off the school bus, they would be unsupervised until she got home much later. We got word of this situation, and invited the children to come over to our house after school. We laughed and played games together, watching Peggy, the oldest, tumble around our living room or outside when it was nice doing routines for her cheerleading. Most of the time, we fed them with our family, but sometimes their mother would bring a dish over. Occasionally, on weekends we would have a barbeque and the six of them would all come over.

Inevitably, there was a divorce, and Fred would have visiting rights. When he had all five for their summer two week visit, Pat decided to use that time for a major clean up of the house. She told me she was going to panel the kids' bedrooms while they were gone, and right away I volunteered to help. With my limited carpentry skills, I had no idea what I was in for. Pat and I went to the lumber yard in Clarence in her little Camaro, and picked out some paneling. The paneling that she selected was out of her budget range, but I found some dry wall with simulated wood paper applied to it. The sales person suggested a glue gun with plenty of glue to adhere the panels to the wall and ceiling. I suggested we get extra in case we needed it rather than having to drive back. The same was true of the molding we picked out. The sales person helped us load the dry wall on the roof of that small Camaro, and we were off to redecorate the rooms. I told her to drive slowly or we would be airborn.

Once we got back, we started to glue the paneling using about one tube per panel. I insisted on that much because I wanted to make sure they were fastened soundly because if they fell down with the kids in bed, it could be a disaster. I went on to suggest that we nail them as well. It took three vacation days for Pat and me to almost finish the rooms. I say almost since the final thing we had to do was put up the ceiling molding. I did not know a thing about a miter box, and thank goodness we bought 50% extra wood for my errors. I cut and re-cut never getting the angles correct. Finally I called our neighbor Deke Kidd who he helped us finish the project. Peggy, Jim, Peter, Janie, and Paul came back to their newly decorated rooms, and were delighted. This made all of the frustrations we went through worth the effort.

It was only a few weeks later as I looked out of our living room window that I saw this pair of legs almost straight out behind a rototiller. It was Pat's mom trying to make a trench to plant a hedge. Both Pat and her mom were very slight of frame – I would guess 102 pounds soaking wet. I told Nancy I would be right back, and then proceeded across the road. I told 'grandma' to shut the motor off so that I could finish the project. While I worked carving out the trench, Pat was going to Wilsey's, the local nursery to get a dozen or so forsythia bushes that I helped to plant in the trench. We thoroughly enjoyed helping this family. A week before we moved to Connecticut, we had Pat and her family over for a nice meal. As we listened to the stereo, the song playing was "Oh, Spanish Eyes", Pat started sobbing. It dawned on me that her ex-husband had run away with a Spanish nun, and that was the reason for the tears, it seemed like a cleansing.

The day before we were moving, Pat introduced us to a very nice man she had met at work, who seemed to blend with her kids very well. When the moving trucks arrived at our house the next day, Pat and her family came over, hugged each one of us, and with tears in her eyes she said, "God placed you here to help us, and I told Him you did a wonderful job". Peggy, Jim, Peter, Janie, and Paul lined up for their good-byes and said, "Thanks a million".

It was only a short time later we received a wedding notice with a note from Pat saying she was now the happiest person in the world.

CONNECTICUT WAS THE NEXT STOP

Our friends, Bob and Jane Hipley, came to visit us when we moved to Hamden, Connecticut. They brought their three year old daughter, Elizabeth, along with them. After the adults fed the kids, we asked our oldest, Laura, to supervise them while we had our dinner. Nancy lit the candles, Jane helped put the food on the table, Bob brought in the steaks, and I poured the wine. Just as we were toasting our friends, Laura came out with a terrified look on her face and said, "Beth disappeared!" We all ran into the other room where I checked to see if she had gone out the window or maybe hid under the bed. Nancy yelled out, "Oh my God, the clothes chute in the closet". She ran down the stairs, weaved her way through a couple rooms, and found Beth at the bottom of the chute. Beth's eyes were as wide as saucers, and they seemed to say, "I swore I was upstairs a few minutes ago". Thank goodness, we had changed the sheets and towels before they came so that they could soften the spot where Beth landed from above. The nine foot drop scared us, but Beth was not hurt. We went back upstairs and put a heavy metal plate over the chute in the closet to prevent any other accidents. The kids continued to play while we toasted again.

Other stories come to mind during the time we lived in Hamden -

- It was mid-December, and our church about three blocks away had a nice nativity on the front lawn. It was three blocks away so we walked there with our children marveling at all the Christmas lights as we walked. That evening when I was tucking Jennifer in bed when she started to cry. I asked her what was wrong, and she said, "Baby Jesus has to be cold out there. Could I give Him my 'blanky'?" I told her what a nice idea that was and bundled her up for the drive back to the crèche where Jennifer hopped out and left her favorite 'blanky' with Jesus in the crib.

- About four doors down from us, there was a sweet elderly lady that was a little senile, but always said hello when I walked by. She had her shrubs decorated with plastic flowers even in the winter, but the yapping dog across the street really got to her. She put a sign in her front window about six feet long and two feet high that said, "SHUT UP DOG". I don't know if she was giving the owners a hint or if she thought the dog could read.

- Peter and Pidgie Knudsen and their five children were our good friends while we lived in Hamden, Connecticut. In the fall they asked us if we wanted to go with them to Cape Cod for the Labor Day weekend. We said we would be delighted, and that long weekend we took off in separate cars since with our brood and theirs we had a total of twelve. It was comical stopping at a restaurant or motel to have someone ask, "How many in your party". When we answered, "twelve", we usually got a very funny look. The Knudsen's owned a dairy so they packed a couple of coolers full of milk, eggs, cheese, bacon, bread, and cereal. On our second night, we had adjoining rooms and like the day before, we cooked a hearty breakfast in our room. I remember Pidgie and Nancy cooking in electric skillets for all of us, ignoring a sign that said "No food or drink allowed in the room". We had the door open to air out the odor from frying the bacon, and even though the aroma must have hit the front desk, the management must have felt sorry for our large group because they never said a word about our cooking. We did get a call from them since the eight kids were going in and out of the doors with a loud bang, bouncing a basketball off the building while the adults were preparing breakfast. At first we thought we were going to get reprimanded for bringing in food, but the manager said, "Please keep the noise down; the banging of the doors and thump, thump, thump of the basketball is annoying the guests". We had a long, lazy weekend with more than a few laughs and some very enjoyable times. Would we do it again? Oh yes we thought at the time . . . maybe in 5 – 10 years.

Charity Begins at Home in Battle Creek, Michigan

Through our church, my wife volunteered to be a telephone reassurance caller. She received a list of people who were shut-in, depressed, lonely, or just needed someone to talk to. One particular woman worked her way right into the hearts of our family. Mrs. Joseph was a widow living on a small social security pension. We decided to "adopt" her, and brought all three of our children with us each time we visited bringing bags of groceries and love. Our children would shop for the groceries with us, they had a voice in what we selected; it was important to please Mrs. Joseph. Nancy and I were setting an example for our children to be aware of the need to help those less fortunate. This, we told them was more important than collecting material things in life.

Mrs. Joseph was always glad to see us, and would greet us with a large smile each time we visited. She loved to rub our children's hair, give each of us a hug, and say what a nice family we had. Her black and white television kept her company when other people were not around. She could not afford a colored one, nor did she need one since she used different strips of colored plastic to cover her screen, making her television appear in color.

Eventually, after a year or more of visits, groceries, and stories, one of Mrs. Joseph's children had her move in with them. As we bid her farewell, she hugged us as though she did not want to let go. When we were leaving, she said, "Thank you for caring so much for me, and remember God will be good to you".

Too often we underestimate the power of touch, a smile, a kind word,
a listening ear, an honest compliment, or the smallest act of caring; all
of which have the potential to turn a life around
– Leo F. Buscaglia

A Big Brother to Twin Boys

There was a campaign on the radio and television stating the dire need for Big Brothers and Big Sisters. Nancy and I decided this would be a good cause helping children from broken homes. It is important to have an adult to look up to and be that role model or Big Brother. I met with the officials and filled out the necessary application. They wanted to know if I was willing to accept more than one little brother because there was such a need. I didn't even hesitate; of course I would! I was assigned twin boys about ten years old with shocks of blond hair named Allen and Ricky. Once a week we did something and I always called in advance to arrange a time to pick them up. Taking them to a movie, out for dinner, or just to letting them play in the park. One time I took them to Shrank's Cafeteria which always had such good food. Both kids piled their plates with chicken, mashed potatoes, green beans, biscuits, and a separate plate of desserts. Somehow there were packets of honey at the end of the line, and Ricky and Allen said they just <u>loved</u> honey. I asked the cashier if I could pay for several extra packets, and she just smiled and said, "Take what you want". The boys were certainly open to that so they stuffed a couple extra into their pants pockets. Ricky must have punctured one as he did this because pretty soon he was dancing around saying how sticky his pant legs were. As we were just about ready to go into the movie, I knew I had to help him with this problem. I found some newspaper on the ground and told Ricky to stuff it into his pants pocket. All we could hear as we walked into the movie was, "crunch, crunch, crunch". The best chuckle I had was that evening when I let the boys out at their home and saw Ricky walking gingerly to avoid the stickiness in his pants.

A couple of weeks later, Binder Park golf course was having a tournament to benefit the Big Brother and Big Sisters organization. Nancy and I signed up, and of course, had a great time even with our limited golf experience. Two things happened that day which are hard to forget. On a 400 plus yard hole, there was a prize for the longest drive. My drive hit a tree close by to the right and ricocheted back about 85 yards. This caused quite a bit of cackling and doubling up with laughter from the bystanders. I simply said, "Maybe I will win for the longest drive backwards". At the banquet afterwards, there was the awarding of prizes and one of them was an announcement for the closest to the pin for the ladies. The name they announced was, "Lynn Miller". I knew on the par 3 my shot was 3' 4" from the pin, but did not check to see which hole was for the ladies. At that point, I just had Nancy go up and get the prize for me. Since it was just a sleeve of golf balls, I could live with that on my conscious.

As the months went by, I was told of the Indian Guides, an organization for boys. This seemed to fit perfectly for Ricky and Allen who seemed excited to be with the group of other boys who met every two weeks. Before the meeting would start, we all stood in a circle holding hands, and one by one a boy would get in the circle and tell the "Great White Father" what good things he had done since the previous meeting. Ricky's turn came and he looked up and said, "I have been a very good boy lately. I helped my mother mow the lawn, empty the garbage, and walk the dog". On the sidelines, Allen would say, "Ricky, you lie. You never walked the dog or did those other things". The same thing happened when it was Allen's turn; whatever he said he had done, Ricky would say, "That is a lie, Allen".

One of our projects was to make a paper-mâché tee-pee out of chicken wire and paste. We had two weeks to make this, and were to meet with the other boys to select the best one. From the beginning, I had little hope that we would be in the top group since I had always been in sales and marketing, not building things. Our tee-pee could have passed for a large hornet's nest like one would see hanging from a tree limb. It was oddly shaped, but we had fun making it. Just before displaying our work of art, Allen noticed that we had forgotten to make a doorway. This was an oversight on my part, so I borrowed some scissors and cut off the top part of the tee pee. I told the twins if anyone asked about the door, to say we did not have a traditional one so we could keep the animals out, and this way too, it was warmer inside. Also, we could say to the other boys who wanted to stop for a bite to eat they could swing by and drop in.

The boys were fun to be with, and they enjoyed the companionship and friendship of our family. After a couple years, the boys moved away to another town with their mother, but I know that my presence in their lives made a difference.

Before getting active with the Big Brothers, I read their mission statement and was impressed. It is:

The mission of Big Brothers and Big Sisters is to make a positive difference in the lives of children and youth primarily through a professionally supported one on one relationship with a caring adult and to assist them in achieving their highest potential as they grow to become responsible men and women by providing committed volunteer leadership and standards of excellence.

THE KENTUCKY DERBY AND FISHING AT HATTERAS

Like many couples in their mid-forties, their kids are old enough to stay home by themselves while the adults have fun and explore new things and places. We decided with our friends Carole and Jim Frohardt that it would be exciting to go to the Kentucky Derby and on to Hatteras, North Carolina. We started making plans in the fall of 1983. Carole's boss at the foundry said he knew a Kentucky Colonel who could meet us and get us tickets. Wanting to make our bets pay handsomely, each couple bought a book on handicapping horses. We compared notes on the jockeys, record, added weight needed, position of the horse in the race, and any other comments like a strong finish in the stretch, or a good horse on a sloppy track. The tickets were $75 each, and seemed quite a bit considering it was 25 years ago. Our plans called for staying in Southern Indiana the night before the race; driving about 50 miles or so to Louisville the day of the race. Our enthusiasm was high because we were prepared having read up on how to be a pro-bettor.

It was Saturday, May 5, 1984. Our instructions from Carole's boss were to meet around 11 am near the paddock, not gathering in a group to look conspicuous. Another couple who we met in Indiana joined us as they wanted to sit with us. We were at the track early having purchased programs to review what horses we would choose to place our money. Most people are unaware that on Derby Day there are ten races with the one that everyone watches on television being the eighth race. Our group of six was like an accordion, first all together then separated as we had been advised. It seemed like hours passed when actually it was just 25 or 30 minutes before a gentleman approached our group and asked if we were the friends from the Foundry in Battle Creek. When we confirmed, he introduced himself as the Colonel, giving us each a wrist band to wear. This would allow us up to the floor where the dignitaries, press, and owners were. The Colonel stopped, glanced around, and said, "Listen, I know the winning horse - his name is Taylor's Special". He went on to say he was with the trainer that morning, and the horse in warm-up had to be held back as witnessed by his slight cut on each side of his mouth.   I don't recall the odds, but believe he was going off at 8-1 which meant a winning $2 ticket would return $18. Money was an object, but when you get the inside information, it wasn't. Our plan was to pool our winnings so each couple from Battle Creek, bought 25 $2 tickets which meant the Frohardt's and we could get a win return of $900. We were told by the Colonel to hold our wrists up as we took the escalator to the reserved area, then he left. Strange, but no one else was showing their bands. We looked like a bunch of proud newborn babies showing off our bands. There were not any seats reserved for us so we figured we could sit anywhere; not so! It dawned on us that we had "been had" so we just sat in available seats with the press from the Chicago Tribune, New York Times, Cleveland Plain Dealer, and well, you get the idea. We were seated only a short time when a lady in a large brimmed hat studded with a diamond pin in the shape of a horse exclaimed we were in her seats. My wife blurted out in a perfect Southern drawl, "Excuse us ma'am, ma husband has made a most terrible error". After a mint julep or two and minor betting on the first 7 races, it was time for the big event with Taylor's Special. When my wife went to the restroom, Carole said, since we had a "sure" winner, she would put up her $50 if I would too. After announcing the horses, seeing them parade in their spectacular colors, and singing 'My Old Kentucky Home', it was post time. They were off. Rounding the last turn on the 1 ¼ mile track our horse was 8th in a field of 20, and finished 13th. We did not lose on the first 7 races as our meager $2 bets made us even. Now we were down $200, and we could kick ourselves for listening to the Colonel and not following the details we read in our books. We didn't bet on the ninth race because we were embarrassed and almost broke, but I read carefully on the 10th, and bet $40 to place on Peanut Butter and Jelly. From our angle, it appeared he was 3rd, so we scampered out to beat the crowd. Outside the gate, we heard the results, and I had won $10.20 for place or $204 on my ticket. I told the rest of the group to stay put and I would redeem my winning ticket. Try fighting a couple hundred thousand people coming out when you are trying to get back in. 'Excuse me, pardon me, yes, I know the race is over'. By the time I reached the window, it was closed, but a person inside slid a paper to me to fill out so the proceeds could be mailed to me later. With my win, I said we would charter a boat to go fishing when we got to Hatteras, North Carolina.

We took our time driving to Hatteras, slept in on Sunday morning, and booked our fishing charter for Monday. It was a cool morning as about twenty of us climbed aboard the "Lady Hatteras". After a 45 minute ride from shore, the captain said we could lower our lines. Just as he was declaring, "No casting from the boat", I had already wound up and cast with my hook, zinging through the air, and finally plunking down. After three to four hours, everyone on the boat caught something except me. I was used to fishing with a large hook, big worm, large bobber, on a quiet stream or river; not bouncing around with nineteen others. The catch for the four of us was ten keepers of various species and size, the plan was to return to our cottage and have a late lunch of fried fish and a big salad. Jim and I had instructions to clean the fish while the gals set the table, made a salad, got drinks, and found a good radio station for good music. After about twenty minutes, we had one fish cleaned and nine to go. Looking around I spotted a fish market across the street and down a few doors. We decided to take our fish there and have the fish in the store matched up with the ones we had. We wrapped our catch up in newspaper taking it to the fish market to explain our situation to the staff. The people at the fish market found this to be hysterical. We killed some time at the market, returning to the cottage where our wives exclaimed what a nice job we had done. They were never told until several years later when Jim just couldn't hold the secret any more. There is an old saying – "Only 2 can keep a secret if one of them is dead".

THE GIFT OF GIVING IS A POWERFUL TOOL – THIS TIME IN UTAH

We moved to Southern Utah in 1996 to prepare for retirement, and it didn't take us long to discover three casinos about 50 miles from our home. About once a month we would venture to Mesquite, Nevada, always with a goal in mind for our winnings. On the second or third visit we decided whatever winnings we had that day would be given to a needy family back in St. George or Hurricane, Utah. After about ten minutes of play, I hit a royal flush on a quarter machine for $1,000, so we got up and left. The next morning after mass I told the priest of my winnings; that we wanted to give the money to a needy family. He said that in our home town of Hurricane, there was a very poor family who had lost a three month old boy, and did not have the money to pay for the funeral. I got the name of the funeral home and contacted them on Monday morning to get the details on the baby boy who passed away. After stopping by to pay for the bill anonymously, I found that the amount needed was $998. My day was good because I helped a family in their time of sorrow.

I Pray that Somebody Adopts Me

No, this was not me. I was given that chance in the orphanage, but the couple that came to size me up told the nuns later that they would pass. I remember being called off the baseball field by Sister Luciana who introduced me to this heavy lady and burly man. I wasn't happy having to leave the baseball game because I was on deck to be the next batter. Sister told me I should not have swung the bat at the gentleman's leg because he said that I looked like a fighter and could be a problem child.

This is a different story however. This is the story of a cat in a shelter…. a fuzz ball with orange and caramel colored fur and eyes that said, "I am alone and scared here. Will you please take me home?" My wife bent over to look closer at this kitten, and a little paw came through the bars and started playing with her necklace. That did it! We had Missy for nine years in Michigan, bringing her with us when we moved to Utah. Missy would ride on my shoulders when I went down the hill to get the mail, and often I would fall asleep with her draped around my neck as I napped in the chair. Her antics made us laugh. One season in Battle Creek I planted some pumpkin seed on the back side of the house. The plants would vine and leaves seem to grow at a very fast pace. Each time Missy would go out the back door things looked different and she would bounce up in the air with great surprise when she saw the changes to the large vine.

When it was time to move to Utah, our nest was empty since our kids were living on their own. It was just Nancy, Missy, and me driving the 2,300 miles or so from Battle Creek, Michigan to Hurricane, Utah. Missy rode on the arm rest between us, and would press her nose as hard as she could on my arm. When a truck would pass, she would shake and sometimes hop over to the back seat or on the back floor. The first motel where we stopped had a sign, "No pets allowed". Further down the road we stopped at another motel that had the same sign; not outside, but directly on the counter. I pretended not to see it and asked for a room in the back that was quiet. After parking, we walked a short distance to our room noticing that the front desk was about 30 doors away. Missy started meowing angrily; I turned slightly so my garment bag hid Missy's carrier. As I did this, I said loudly enough for the clerk to hear, "Nancy, I've got a band-aid and medicine to put on your fingers. Don't cry; I didn't mean to slam the car door on them".

We made the trip in 3½ days, and were relieved to be in our new home. We had been settled only a few months when Missy who was always used to exploring the outdoors in Michigan went outside one day and never came back. We had rewards posted and her picture put in the paper, but our veterinarian called and said no doubt a coyote had gotten her. It took him three cats after moving here from Colorado to figure out that is what happens here in the desert.

Nancy and I just held each other as we sobbed and sobbed. She said, "I don't think I ever want to have another cat; Missy is irreplaceable". Just a few months later, she was walking in our neighborhood on the sidewalk above the golf course to go visit her friend, Jan, when all of a sudden a scrawny orange emaciated kitten with one eye closed ran from between the houses right into Nancy's arms and our lives. I was at my computer when she came downstairs and said, "Look what I found or I should say, what found me". I replied, "I thought you said you never wanted another cat". To this she said, "I did say that, but this little kitten is different; he needs us". He turned out to be different all right! We named him "Duffer" since he was running from the golf course when Nancy found him. His purr was like having a V-12 engine running in the garage with the doors shut. The very next day we made an appointment with our vet, and to our surprise, he said that our little one pound kitten had to be around five months old; he definitely was starving. I stocked up on baby food like lamb and gravy, beef and barley, kitten dry food, and people food too like eggs and tiny shrimp. The vet gave us some medicine for his eye, gave Duffer some shots, and we made another appointment to have him neutered.

We could see that he had some street-smarts having been on his own. After he gobbled down his food and purred with thanks, I walked him down to his potty box, scratched the litter with his paw, and said, "Now Duffer, this is where you go when you have to go". About an hour later after his potty training lesson, I watched as Duffer went down the stairs, and I could hear him scratching in the litter box. I may have been a good teacher, but he was a prize student!

SOMETIMES A BARGAIN IS NOT A BARGAIN

It was Saturday, March 16, 1999, the day before St. Patrick's Day. At the supermarket, I bought a shamrock plant that had lots of clovers and many white blossoms. At the check-out, I showed the cashier the plant and said this shamrock is wilted and kind of sick looking and asked if I could get a discount. She did not even hesitate and lowered the price from $3.99 to $2.99. When I got home, I watered the plant and put it on the window sill. In a matter of a few hours, it had sprung to life with leaves and flowers in a perky condition. I was proud of my bargaining skills until . . .

Sunday morning we noticed the flowers were all gone and Duffer's eyes were rolling around and his stomach was bulging. We immediately called the vet and told him the whole story. He said to come to his office in a half hour; the exact time it took me to drive from Hurricane to St. George. The vet said the toxicity of the clover blossoms caused Duffer's stomach to bloat, and he would try using some charcoal tablets to absorb the gas. Since we discovered the discomfort right away, he did not think he would need to operate. He did say however, that he would need to stay over a night or two. I called on Tuesday to check on my buddy, and the office said I could pick him up Wednesday morning. Granted, I saved a dollar on the forlorn plant, but I could have bought 100 as the bill I was presented was $323.00. The moral of the story is: a shamrock may bring you luck provided you don't have a cat that chews off the blossoms.

Now when we get flowers for special occasions, we spray them with soapy water, place them on the table only at dinner time, and they go in the back bedroom with the door shut. The very best solution is not to buy flowers at all. We figured as a little kitten growing up on his own in the desert, Duffer had to fend for himself. His diet was probably grasses and plants, and no doubt, his eye got jabbed from a cactus or desert animal. So as a treat, we do allow him to chew on the leaves of pineapple, the green tops of strawberries, or wheat grass we buy just for him since he is who he is.

Animals Have Souls Just Like Us

I often imagine tiny little Duffer hiding in sagebrush for protection saying a prayer that may have gone like this:

Oh, good Lord, I can't make it much longer on my own

I don't have much to eat, and I am so hungry and all alone

Some days I wish I just had a baby brother

I don't know my father or my mother

Some people just dropped me off from their car

Each night I hide from coyotes in this desert war

So I beg you, God, to hear my plea

It's tough out here with only one eye to see

If I had a home, I could purr and play

If you just give a chance to this tiny little stray

After being baptized with the name of Duffer, he later had his confirmation, and he agreed on his middle name of Patrick. For a special Christmas gift his first year in our home, we made him a stocking to hang by the fireplace. It is made of red felt, trimmed with white fake fur, his name written in sparkle paint, several white mice on the toe, and the date 1998 is there too.

ELEPHANTS, HIPPOS, TIGERS, AND MONKEYS

It seems every day some past story comes up . . . here is one I had forgotten about until recently when my wife said she woke up laughing in the middle of the night after remembering it. It was Saturday, April 21, 2000, I was at our daughter's apartment in Livonia, Michigan, where my wife, Nancy, daughters Laura and soon to be bride Jennifer, all met. They were discussing gifts to purchase for the bridal party and other things for the upcoming wedding. I asked where I could get a haircut while they were shopping, and both girls said I could walk three blocks left, two blocks up, and then three blocks to the right where there was an upscale hair salon on the second floor of a large mall. Better yet, they suggested I cut straight across the field in front of the apartment and shave my walking time in half.

After some morning chatter and another cup of coffee, I decided to journey across the field. Since our daughters could not recall the name of the salon, upon arriving at the mall, I asked and was directed to Daniel's Hair with a Flair. As I entered the salon, a young well-tanned, slightly built gentleman wearing black leather pants, a white long-sleeved shirt, and a black leather vest, glided across the room, swiveling his hips while approaching. He said, "How lovely to see you. Who is the person attending to you today?" When I told him I did not have an appointment, he threw up his hands and said, "Oh, but hon forgive me, we are completely booked......this is Saturday you know!" I mentioned that I was in desperate need as tonight was the rehearsal dinner. He took my hand and walked me to the door. He said there was a shop downstairs that could possibly accommodate me. I was given specific directions, and as I asked about this place to be sure they would be able to help me he almost laughing sputtered, "I am so very positive". Thanking him I was reaching in my pocket for a tip, but something told me, "not yet".

I proceeded down the stairs, took a right turn, and four doors down found Paula's Precious Moments. Before going in I checked a dozen shops on each side, and decided this must be the place. As I entered, a princess with butterfly wings and a wand whispered, "Please follow me". She took me to the counter, and was going into detail about the various settings for baby's first haircut. Her name was Candy and she obviously had confused me with someone who had called inquiring about particulars. I tried to interrupt several times thinking this would be interesting for some other dad or granddad. The prices quoted depended on how memorable you wanted that first haircut or as she called it, angel's snippings to be. You had a choice for your child to sit on an elephant, hippo, tiger, or monkey while getting their first cut. Allowing the little one to select which one he or she felt most comfortable with. The base price was $15, and included a clown taking an 8x10 picture framed and signed something like "Tommy's or Sally's first". An added treat with each animal seat was a tray with M&M's, chocolate milk, and several balloons.

When the sales-pitch was over, I told Candy what a great job she did, but I needed a favor. I needed a haircut, but did not want to be on display to the hundreds of people going by. She said, "The tallest animal . . . ", I interrupted her and said, "Please no animal. Don't you have a back room with some privacy. All of a sudden, Paula came over and said, "I could not help but overhear your conversation. I suggest you use the sound-proof crying room that we use for kids who are afraid". I said, "I'll take it", and "Please, please, please don't open the door while you are cutting my hair". A tiny princess by the name of Scarlet cut my hair and we both were laughing . . . this was a first for this room. Before I left, Rhoda, one of the clowns, asked if I wanted my picture taken. I laughingly declined. She said they could autograph it Grandpa's unique experience in the crying room. They were all clapping, even the little tykes, when I left with Paula saying, "You are a cut above the rest".

Not only growing up, but a practice I try to maintain today –Don't be afraid to release the child with your soul
– anonymous

SOME THINGS
JUST DON'T COME
NATURALLY...

"Tell me and I'll forget, show me and I may remember, involve me, and I'll understand"
— Chinese proverb

Usually, I was told I did it wrong; what a nitwit brain for trying to fix or build anything. With that information drilled into my head while growing up, is there any wonder why, back in my formative years, I botched up quite a bit? My mishaps and struggles continued even into my adult life with a few specific examples coming to mind.

DRIVING LESSONS

Before I ever bought a shirt, slacks, or any other article of clothing, I checked the label and read the washing instructions very carefully. For example, if the label said 100% cotton, I would always buy one size larger to allow for shrinkage, and knew it had to be ironed. Later I got smarter and started choosing fabrics with some polyester for easy maintenance. Now why couldn't I pay as much attention when driving somewhere? I decided "practice makes perfect", and no practice could make for a possible disaster. My college roommate, Jeff, told me if I ever wanted to borrow his car, I could. Sheepishly, I told him that I did not know how to drive, and he was floored. Daly's had ingrained in us that we could not get a driver's license or get married until we were 21 without their permission. Jeff, bless his heart, said he had access to the questions on the driver's test, and would rehearse them with me for a couple weeks. Also he told me he would teach me what I needed to learn about driving a car. So he began lessons with me, in parking, obeying speed limits, entering and exiting freeways, and the placement of the wheel when parking downhill. I made an appointment for my driver's test and passed both the driving and the written test with ease. Thank you Jeff!

When I got engaged to Nancy, I drove her to the Daly's house in her parent's car to make the introductions. With Nancy reading the map, it was easy getting to La Grange from Columbus. To say the least, the Daly's were shocked. Where on earth did you learn how to drive? I think they knew better than to ask how I had dared to learn without their permission.

After getting married and having to drive on my own, the challenges began. I have always admitted I was not mechanically blessed, and after all, the car is mechanical, and my being at the wheel was no help. When I was dating Nancy, I knew she lived on Fallis Road which was off of Indianola Avenue, in a neighborhood where the houses all looked similar. More often than not, I would ring the wrong doorbell. There were several college girls that lived in the area, and when I would come to the door, I would hear, "Lynn, Nancy is three doors down". In the case of arriving at Sally's, she would laugh and say, "You passed her house again, she is five doors down".

After graduating from college, one of my first sales calls was in Indianapolis, Indiana. I somehow got confused on a cloverleaf and ended up in Zanesville, Ohio. This was quite a bit east, but I always allowed sufficient time between calls to get lost.

No doubt the most embarrassing time was the day the president of the company wanted to make a few calls with me to several of the large accounts in upstate New York. I was trying to impress Dave by going just on memory, and after circling and weaving around town, he asked if I was lost. He swore we had passed the Shell station and the hardware store before. Quickly, I said, "Well, you know in a town of this size and since they were chain stores, there are probably more than one of each". After a few miles and what seemed like forever, I told him I knew a shortcut and drove down a dirt road which was a dead end overlooking a gravel pit. All Dave said was, "My gosh, you are something else". At least, the calls went well and he was impressed with my sales presentation. The driving was different!

During my first 18 years of life, I was never more than 20 miles from the foster home where I lived. Getting to Ohio State University was a 125 mile hitchhike. Once I graduated, my territory with the company began with two states, then six, and finally added four

Canadian provinces.   Eventually, as Worldwide Director of Sales, I travelled and was responsible for 43 countries.   Did I get lost? Never! I found a way around that. Sales managers and distributors met me at the airport and took me around.

BEING NEIGHBORLY

I always felt that the neighbors thought we were pretty good people; always willing to help, kept our children safe in our fenced yard, and played our music softly. We had flowers, trees, a neatly painted house, never drove around the neighborhood fast, and most importantly, had a green, green, dandelion-free yard.

Our next door neighbors, the Messemer's, were a little older than us and recently married. He was a policeman and she worked in an office. Harold was frantically digging dandelions out of his yard with one of those pronged tools. I yelled over the fence that I had just finished spraying my lawn for dandelions, and I could get some more "killer" for him which would save him a lot of time and effort. I even offered to spray the lawn for him since the hose and jar were already hooked up, but more importantly, they were getting ready to leave on a weekend vacation. At the nursery, I grabbed a red and yellow container off the same shelf where I had gotten mine. I rushed home, poured the liquid in the jar, hooked it up, and proceeded to spray their yard. When I finished, I was rinsing out the jar, and noticed on the container the word "Erase". All of the sudden I had a bad feeling, and upon reading further, realized that it would permanently wipe out weeds, or anything green including grass. The more I read what this powerful product could do, the more of an uneasy feeling I got. I told Nancy what had happened, and she said that I must tell them as soon as they got back. She also suggested I bring Laura and Jennifer with me to help soften the blow. After all, he was a policeman who carried a gun! I rehearsed what I was going to say a couple of times, and then sheepishly went over to their house when they got home Sunday night. Before I could even finish the sentence, he said, "Let me guess. You put something different on by mistake, like grub killer. That's okay because your intentions were good". I blurted out, "But this is not okay. The store had the same red and yellow colored package as mine on the same shelf, but it is Erase which is going to make your entire lawn disappear". I told him I had taken the empty containers back to the nursery to show them the similarity in packaging, even though they were quite different products. The manager said someone had misplaced the package, and it was their mistake. I was told to water it well, and the brown cast that was already showing up could green up if watered thoroughly. The assistant manager said he had heard my story, and that the store would provide grass seed, topsoil, and whatever it took to put the lawn in tip-top shape. Slowly the lawn started coming back, and after a month, it was like new. It was even free of dandelions! We were still good neighbors. Facing the problem as soon as it arose was the best thing to happen. I told the truth, was sorry, and rectified the error.

A Handyman I'm Not...

One story would be the time I tried to put up a cup dispenser in the bathroom of our first home. I had never heard of studs in a wall; the only studs I knew were all my fraternity brothers. However, they were not around when I started pounding away at our bathroom wall. I kept trying to find something that would make the nail hold and finally scored when I hit something solid, known as a stud. That was thirteen holes later. As I counted all of them trying to decide what to do, I got a brilliant idea to cover them with decals. A trip to the store allowed me to find just what I needed – a colorful fish with bubbles. Once home, I applied them to the wall there they covered the holes, giving our little bathroom some personality.

Trying to make life easier for my wife who was pregnant with our second child and already having an infant to look after, I thought I would take a stab at putting a clothes chute in the bathroom. While Nancy grocery shopped, I decided to surprise her, and I certainly did! Cutting a square under the "zink" wasn't too difficult unless you had copper pipes directly in your cutting line. At first, I thought the builder must have used good oak or thick wood because the sawing was not going too well. Although I was sweating profusely, the saw was sweating too, as I noticed the moisture on the blade. Upon further review, I discovered a nick in the copper pipe that was dripping slowly but steadily. I hurriedly got a towel to dry the pipe and put some chewing gum and a band-aid on the pipe cut. The next thing I did was call a plumber to fix the pipe. After a redesign, my clothes chute design changed from a square to a rectangle. All that my wife said when she returned from shopping and saw the chute and heard my plight was, "Maybe you should limit your expertise to yard work where you are really good".

Now the neighbors and our friends had to agree, I had the greenest grass in the county. One reason for this it that I had invested in one of those sprinklers that travelled along the hose regardless of how I directed its path. It was about 11 p.m. one night when our neighbor called quite upset. He informed me that my sprinkler had gotten stuck and the water was shooting right into their bedroom window. I apologized profusely, mentioning what a dumb thing I had done and the only response I heard through the phone was, "You got that right!"

At our modest home in Hamden, Connecticut, we had an outdoor faucet that dripped constantly. I had most things done around the house like painting, pruning, and yard work but that faucet kept on dripping. I tried several times to turn the knob tighter with no luck. Finally, I got a pipe wrench and after a few turns, the drip stopped. The next day after lunch we decided to go to the beach for a swim. Before leaving, I suggested to the children that it would be a long drive and everyone needed to go "potty". Our middle child, Jennifer, came to the car where I was waiting and said, "You know what, daddy, we don't have to go to the beach, we can swim in the basement". Oh my, I thought, as I went inside to see. The water downstairs was a few inches deep from that pipe I had twisted which caused it to break. To make things even worse, this occurred during a holiday weekend and the plumber charged extra, but he got it fixed. Derek Bok said it best - *There is nothing more dangerous than ignorance in action.*

THE WILDLIFE AND A WILD SÉANCE

Our Michigan home offered plenty to see as the wildlife was prevalent around and behind our house. Our home sat on a hill with about an acre of yard and woods. Behind that was a continuation of the woods which covered about five acres with a stream flowing through it. I fed the birds, squirrels, rabbits, and deer usually starting in the fall and throughout the winter until about May when there were abundant seeds and berries growing in the woods. The suet feeder attracted several kinds of woodpeckers like the Red-Bellied, Downy, or Northern Flicker. At the window feeders there was always a flurry of yellow and purple finch, chickadees, nuthatch, sparrows, and cardinals. On the ground, the doves scrambled for seeds that were dropped or scratched out of the feeder. Sometime between Halloween and Thanksgiving, I would go to the orchards and buy or get free, five to six bushels of cull apples. The smaller trees in the woods around our home lost their leaves quickly showing off their bare limbs. I would take the apples I had gotten from the orchards, and one by one, pierce the branches with the fruit. Before long the "apple" trees would need to be loaded again. The deer loved this, and almost every Spring would strut by our picture window. There would be mom, dad, and most often, a few "Bambies" in tow. I have always believed that the way we treat animals is the way we treat people. If we are compassionate, talk softly, greet and touch them gently, both animal and man respond with a happy heart.

At one of the nurseries I had visited I saw a device that was placed in bird bath water that kept the temperature of the water at 45 degrees even if the weather was much colder than that. I purchased it, plugged it into an extension cord, and placed the cord on the

194

ground until it reached the electrical outlet on the back of our house; a distance of about 100 feet. It was really exciting watching the birds drinking from the steaming water. This didn't last long however; after a shaking experience in the dining room and from above.

We usually ate our evening meal around 5:30 to accommodate the activities in which our teenagers were involved; cheerleading, track, football, art, dance, and others. After our prayer before meals, we would always remember Nancy's parents who had died. It seemed every time we would turn the light on in the dining room, it would dim. Even more so when we were praying for the repose of their souls, the light would dim and then go bright. This would happen every night, and we would look up at the overhead fixture with 8-10 Christmas style bulbs. Nancy finally said, "Look, Grandma is with us, and she is okay and just trying to say she loves us all". One particular night it appeared Grandma was reprimanding me for something, but I didn't know what. Every time I touched or bumped the fixture, I got a severe shock and could see and hear sparks. We shut the light off after dinner, and I made a point to call an electrician the next morning. It didn't take long for him to come out, and he right away noticed the orange extension cord for the bird bath to the back of the house. He examined the device and unplugged the unit. There was moisture running down the cord right into where the plug goes into the outlet. We were told the moisture was shorting out the circuit and he was glad we caught it in time or we could have had a really serious electrical fire!

Thank you Mother, thank you Grandma, thank you La Mere!

MY GRILLING EXPERIENCES
SEEMED TO FOLLOW ME

Ohio:

I am certain I had mentioned to my mother-in-law even before I married her daughter that my ability to assemble things was terrible. Perhaps, she was just testing my mechanical skills or she really wanted to see for herself and then say, "You certainly weren't kidding". For my birthday in the "fall", she presented me with a grill which was very thoughtful because I loved to cook out. The only problem was that it was not assembled. I took a few deep breaths, got out my limited tools, and read the instructions somehow knowing this was not going to work. Let's see, "Place each leg one at a time flat to the surface and with a crescent wrench tighten the bolt with a washer outside the grill bowl. Hold bolt firmly turning it slowly from the inside. While tightening, apply another wrench on the outside". The wooden tray that holds the cooking utensils and food was to be assembled next. The brackets on each side are contoured to the grill shape and are held with small screws that have a cap so that the grill or a person will not get scratched. Tap the caps gently, but firmly and . . . that was enough! I had not even gotten to the part about the lid, underlying tray, or positioning of the racks. I kept my cool mumbling some swear words to myself. I then loaded the parts and pieces back into the box it came in and carried it to the street for the trash man to pick up. Wouldn't you know, the next morning my mother-in-law came over. When she saw the grill at the curb she was livid. After gathering it up she took it back to the store telling the clerk that neither she nor her "handicapped" son-in law could assemble it; asking politely if they would please help. The clerk said it was not their policy, but under the circumstances, they would do it for a nominal ten dollars. It was well worth it, and I was sure that I reimbursed my mother-in-law.

New York:

After adding Michigan, Kentucky, and Ontario, Canada to my territory, I had another opportunity to expand my sales when the New York and Eastern shore representative was fired. I volunteered to take the territory providing I could rent, at the company's expense, a place in upstate New York. This made more sense than flying from Ohio to the large key accounts I had just accepted. The vice president of sales said it made sense to him also so we closed our house in Ohio for the summer and got a nice cottage on one of the Finger Lakes. We very often had guests including the in-laws, friends from Ohio, and one weekend a couple we knew from college came by. It was then that I went to the local store to buy several pounds of hamburgers to grill along with chips, pickles, and baked beans. The burger patties seemed fatty, and my suspicions were right, as one by one the burgers flared up, and upon trying to turn them they would fall apart and drop into the coals. Starting with 20 patties, I was down now to 14, then 8, then 2, and finally I shut off the grill to go get some chicken – already cooked.

Michigan:

Soon after arriving from Connecticut, we decided to go to the pool where we had recently acquired a membership. The grill that came with the house had a spit so Nancy and I decided to put a couple of chickens on the spit over low heat while our family went swimming for a couple of hours. Upon arriving back home, all seemed fine as there wasn't any smoke coming from the grill. But when I opened the lid to check our dinner there wasn't any chicken either! After 2 ½ hours of going round and round, there were just charred bones left!

Michigan again:

Nancy and I were at the Frohardt's playing bridge; just Carole, Nancy, and myself. Jim was off with another guy building something. Notice I was not included with the "building men". It was decided we would put a couple of ducks on the grill, play cards while they cooked, and in a couple of hours when Jim returned, we would eat. Three handed bridge with a dummy hand wasn't great, but it passed the time especially with some cold beer. We were enjoying ourselves when we heard some pounding on the glass of the window, and then heard Jim say, "You dumb fools"! We looked out to see the flames from the grill that were almost up to the porch ceiling. We forgot how greasy ducks can be, and without a pan beneath them, the fat just fueled the flames. Jim grabbed a bucket of water and doused the flames. We took the burned ducks into the house. They certainly were done! Slowly we peeled off the blackened skin, and "Holy Smoke", the meat was moist and delicious. We had a great dinner, but rest assured the next time we grilled duck, we used a pan underneath and watched them carefully.

Utah:

First, you should know I haven't burned a thing while in Utah. A very strange thing happened though. We had a grill with a spit, and I had done two chickens to perfection. When they were done cooking I shut the gas off and before bed, after the grill had cooled I put on the cover. About a week later, I invited one of the neighbors over for a cigar and a few beers. He kept on saying that we must have a coyote around our house, in fact, it was close by. We continued sitting and chatting, and after the third beer, Brent got up and exclaimed, "The coyote is really close, like in the bushes off the porch." He came back after searching, stopped, took the cover off the grill, and there was the "coyote". It was the grill spit going round and round with a squeaky noise. I had forgotten to shut it off in my excitement of not burning the chicken.

CAREER

Focusing on a Career

I had worked many long hours ever since my first job as an eighth grader. From then until I finished college, I worked at one job or another so I was not going to waste even one day looking for a job after graduation. My goal was to have one waiting for me. Half way through my junior year, I started checking the newspaper, usually on Sunday, where there would be announcements of conventions coming to town. There was a convention for the insurance industry, the Potato Chip Institute, the Farm Bureau, and the florist and orchard industry to name a few. I re-worked my schedule so I could attend these conventions. I wanted to hear what qualities the firms were looking for, what subjects were important to them, and get a feel for business. There was little trouble getting a badge to attend the shows where various firms had their exhibits. I made it a point to have a neatly pressed suit, hair trimmed, nails clean and cut, and shoes shined. Approaching a convention person, I would introduce myself as a college student who wanted to get some business tips. Never was I turned down, and most of the time, I got invited to lunch or dinner. Around mid-November of 1960, there was a Mid-West Food Convention in town. Dr. Gould suggested we have a booth there with a cross section of products packed in the Midwest. The booth was a hit with colorful, nicely displayed products, and while there I made some very good contacts. I mentioned I would be free after finals during the Christmas break, which was December 10 to January 3. Several firms who showed an interest in me included Del Monte, Stouffers, Green Giant, Frito-Lay and the U.S. Government. I mentally scratched most of them off my list since they were looking for a lab technician or people to be based in house. I knew I did not want to work for the government considering the Gettysburg Address has 226 words, the Ten Commandments has 296 words, and the U.S.D.A., which sets the price, quality, and standards for cabbage had in excess of 15,000 words! My experience with labs, gauges, colorimeters and things that go chinky-chink or puff-puff were almost like a foreign language to me. Soluble solids, titratable acids, and spectrograph readings sent chills down my spine.

Bud Nicholay of the Frito-Lay family invited me to dinner and spoke of production plants making forty tons of potato chips or Fritos per shift. It sounded like another quality control job, and I crossed that off when he said I would be loading or unloading box cars of product. I politely declined saying I had plenty of manual work experience, and wanted to work in marketing or sales where I could be with people. He said that could come later; currently they were at capacity in the sales area. Another time, I was invited to dinner where I was seated with eight businessmen. One gentleman named Carl asked me when I would be graduating. I told him June 1961, handing him one of my homemade business cards. Carl had a large territory covering all of the Midwest selling vegetable seed to the food processors. He was spread too thin with his hub in Wisconsin alone counting for millions of dollars.

A few days after the convention, I got a call from Asgrow's headquarters in New Haven, Connecticut requesting an interview with me anytime between the 10th and 20th of December. At their request, I got an itemized cost for food, air fare, hotel, and taxi, and in a few days had a check in the mail to cover the amount. During the Christmas break, I made the trip and was impressed with the warm welcome from the officers and staff. One very obvious thing I noticed was the average age in the office was late forties, and I would be 21 when I graduated. I could smell success if I worked hard and sold well. I had good experience at least in the 'working' department. After several interviews, the senior vice-president, Dave Behrent, said they would like me to join their team after graduating. I would earn $450 per month, have a company car, and all expenses paid. From previous job offers, this was the lowest by far, but I realized I could climb the success ladder quite rapidly with age on my side. As I was leaving the office, I could hear various voices saying, "Welcome aboard, see you soon, and happy holidays". Dave asked me if I was going home for the holidays and rather than get into the real story, I said, "Yes". I also told him how lucky I felt that day and thanked him.

The real story of course was that once I left the foster home, I returned only twice for a short one or two day visit. While the rest of the fraternity left to be with their families for Christmas, I worked in the lab, and stayed in the fraternity where I had the whole house to myself. My fiancé would invite me over for dinner; her mother was a superb cook. Not only dinners, but how could I forget the breakfasts, two eggs cooked in bacon grease, bacon, English muffins, peanut butter, orange juice, and coffee. Nancy's dad Norm was a character, always joking he would start to tell something then ask me to tell the rest of the story. One time, his wife Sylvia made a banana cream pie which was quite runny. She said, "Now, Lynn, you are in food tech, how do I get the pie to firm up?" I came right back with, "You fill the sink half full of cold water, put in a tray of ice cubes, and soak the bananas for 20 minutes; no longer, no shorter". Norm had to leave the room he was laughing so hard.

SALES CALLS AND OPPORTUNITIES

I recall my first sales call as though it were yesterday, but 47 years have passed since then. A slogan the Proctor and Gamble company used years ago, "You do not get a second chance to make a first impression" was always on my mind those first few years. I studied my 'company Bible' enough times to know most of the material by heart. Feeling confident with a zero share of market with this firm left a broad margin for improvement! After listening intensely, I took notes on what the customer had and wanted. I delivered my best, but had to leave the way I entered, without an order. On the way back to my hotel, I was going over my first sales call and remembered some of the key points of our product I forgot to mention. Turning around, I headed back to finish my presentation concentrating on the things the customer wanted. The result was an order for $1,500, and the customer actually thanked me for returning. I was singing all the way back, and said a simple, "Thank you God".

In Leo Buscaglia's words – Your talent is God's gift to you. What you do with it is your gift back to God

I don't remember any serious failures in life, but a few disappointments along the way allowed me to bounce back with resilience because I had so much practice growing up. One of the largest customers in Michigan divided his purchases equally among several companies. It was one of those rare days when I was in my office that I got the blasting phone call I will always remember. The product our customer ordered was shipped into another country and was to arrive no later than March 10th. It was actually shipped out on that date, arriving twelve days later! The irate customer said that he was shipping our material back, and we would be crawling back to get an order IF we ever got another one. This left a significant impression on me and was woven into many of our sales meetings; "Success is the sum of details".

I chided the salesperson because he needed to accept responsibility for his work ethics telling him that we had work to do. I told him that I would make the first visit to see if I could calm the customer down. Two days after receiving my verbal whip-lashed, I drove to the company. The owner came out of his office, slammed the door of my car shut before I could fully open it, and said "You get out of here now because I am in NO mood for you". I waited a few weeks before deciding to make another visit, and although I had a cool reception, at least I was able to get out of the car. I told the salesperson it might be best that I suture the wounds inflicted on this good and very large account. On my sixth visit in 2½ months, I found the customer fuming over some mix-up in what he had ordered from our competitor. A voice told me to extend my hand and say, "Let me help you. I have all day and will even come back tomorrow and as many days as needed until you feel the problem is solved". It took almost 2½ years, but the initial $200,000, sales volume which had fallen to zero, increased dramatically to over one million dollars.

Life is not easy for any of us. But what of that? We must have perseverence and above all confidence in ourselves. We must believe we are gifted for something, and this thing, at whatever cost, must be attained. -Marie Curie

CONSULTANTS AND TUPPERWARE WEDGEWOOD

I was absolutely thrilled when the president of our company asked me at the tender age of 26 if I would sit in on a discussion with the top management and four consultants from New York. The meeting centered around the South American countries of Brazil and Argentina regarding our entry into the vast soy bean market, and why we should get involved there. I couldn't help but think of what the company was paying these four "stuff-shirts" in comparison to my meager salary. Our president, three vice-presidents, and I sat on one side of the table, and the New York brains sat on the other. We were invited to interrupt with questions during the presentation which I did to their dismay, or should I say, embarrassment. When they gave the acreage of both countries, I asked where they got their information and how often the census was taken? Dr. Craghill, the lead brain had the gall to say that he did not see the relevance of the question so I gave him a short course in statistics. I said, "Let us suppose that the census is taken every ten years, and we are in the 10th year, the information you just presented could be very obsolete". As the discussion continued, I got even more anxious to challenge these whiz kids. When they said there were X thousand acres, I suggested they could be off quite a bit since I believed those two countries used hectares which is 2 ½ times an acre. My side of the table got a big chuckle out of that! The consultants nervously continued, and my homework on those markets was paying off. I was kind to let them jabber for a while then I would ask about the stability of the governments, who owned the land – farmers or government, co-operatives, and the strength of the currencies. The meeting lasted about 45 minutes which had to seem like hours for our guests. Afterwards the president and senior vice-president called me into their offices. I could see how proud of me they were. They suggested that I must have really done my research to come up with such interesting and meaningful questions. The president asked if I would join his wife and him for dinner that evening. Of course, I was flattered, accepted, and drove to his house where his wife, Irma, had various cheeses, nuts, dip, and crackers. Dave suggested, and I agreed to have a martini before dinner – a first for me. I was very impressed with their beautiful home, antique and Chinese accessories, the furniture, and other décor. One of the things that caught my eye was the vast array of blue and white decorative pieces scattered throughout the house, some were even in a special cabinet. There were vases, little boxes, plates, candle holders, trays, saucers, ashtrays, and round, deeper dishes. All I knew or remembered about the blue and white pottery was that my wife received something I thought looked similar once, for buying $25 worth of Tupperware. As I learned later, ours was an imitation piece, made of inexpensive ceramic. After the second heavy martini, I got my courage up and said to Irma, "My word, Irma, you must have gone crazy buying Tupperware". She looked at Dave with a funny expression, and asked why I would say such a thing. At first, I thought maybe she did not want Dave to know how much she spent at the Tupperware party. When I related my story they both laughed at my innocence (and ignorance), but said they understood. Later, at dinner, I asked them to tell me more about their pottery. Irma could see my interest was real, and relayed that the pottery they owned was "Wedgewood", and that it was synonymous with highly coveted, English ornamental china, and one of the oldest patterns dating back more than 240 years. It was sought after for its beauty and intrinsic value. Who said, "Ignorance is bliss"?

I Got Stiffed in Des Moines

Asgrow, the company for which I worked, had research farms scattered all over the world. In Des Moines, Iowa, the heart of farmland country, was one of these such areas that I visited often. This location allowed us to get a Midwest view of promising new vegetable varieties that could handle an average of 35 inches of rain per year, unlike Twin Falls, Idaho, where rainfall was scarce.

It seems like I spent a lot of time there in early summer as the fields would flood. I was there three years in a row during one period. It was during this time that I had put in a long day looking at which crops were salvageable and deciphering crop pedigrees with our researchers. That evening, a group of us decided to go to one of the better restaurants in town. My dinner started with a Chardonnay, then another, and with my filet, mushrooms, and mashed potatoes I had a glass of Cabernet. The meal was great, and took a couple hours as we talked about the risks and benefits of our research farm in Des Moines. After dinner, the rest of the group was going to a strip bar, something that never turned me on. I wasn't a prude, I just wasn't interested. I bid farewell and told them I would walk the two to three miles to the motel because I needed the exercise. About half way home, my walk was interrupted by a young man. He said that Rolly's had a half-court basketball court in their bar, and that they needed one more player. At first I hesitated, and then agreed as long as they took some breaks because in my 30's, I wasn't in the same physical shape as when I was in my 20's. I went into the bar, and was immediately handed a beer. I took off my white shirt, met all the players, and ran up and down the court to loosen up. We played about ten minutes, took a beer break, and played some more. More than once I was told I was pretty good with my ball handling, passing, and faking. At one of the six or so breaks, I was asked how old I was, and when I said, "33" several said for an older guy I had some young moves, and obviously had played before. It was now around 11:30 p.m., and I told the guys I had to go because I had a plane to catch in the morning. I got cooled off walking the half mile left to my room. When I got there, I asked the desk clerk to make sure I got a wake- up call at 7:30 a.m. because my plane left at 9:30 a.m. If I didn't answer, please call again.

The next morning when the phone rang, I was in for the surprise of my life . . . I could not move. I mean, my hands, my feet, and my entire body was like a board. I couldn't answer the wake-up call and just laid there in bed thinking I must have gotten polio overnight. I was really scared. After several calls attempting to wake me, the clerk was knocking at my door along with a security guard. I yelled that I was paralyzed; I could not move. Thank goodness, I had not chained the door. In a few minutes security had it opened and asked me all the details of my condition. When seeing that I could not move, he called for a doctor. When the doctor arrived, I was sputtering about my young wife and three children; how I was just starting my career, and it just wasn't fair that such a bad thing crept up on me while I was sleeping. I told the doctor my story from the beginning, and was so relieved to hear that I would be all right. The doctor thought that my running up and down the court while not in training tightened my muscles, although all the wine, beer, and smoky bar had not helped either. He gave me some muscle relaxers, and said that I should be better later in the day. I was told to get some rest, and not to worry. Next, I asked the security guard if he would cancel my flight, book the same one for the following day, tell the motel clerk that I would be staying another night, and to hang a "do not disturb" sign on my door. It seemed like forever, but in a couple of hours, I was able to move my arms and legs, and right away called home to say I would be home a day late. Nancy asked if everything was okay, and I said, "Yes; some unexpected things came up". When I got home I revealed to her how bad it really was.

For a guy of 33, I had some good moves on the court but if my teammates could have seen me the next morning at 7:30, they may have said, "The old goat just couldn't take it". *None are as old as those who have outlived enthusiasm* – Henry David Thoreau

Taking the Kids on a Business Trip

Sometimes, I would take the children travelling with me. Each one would get a turn so that Nancy could have a break. Once, I had a trip scheduled to Toronto, Canada, and decided to take our three year old daughter, Laura, with me. At her age, the flight from Cleveland was absolutely free. Nancy packed Laura's suitcase, and I put it in the car with mine because we had to get up early for the drive to Cleveland. At the airport in Cleveland, I got a porter to help with the bags so that I could carry Laura whom I thought was sleeping in the backseat. There were two nice soft blankets put on the backseat, but Laura was not there. The problem was I had left Laura at home. I called Nancy who was not too upset because my intentions were good.

A year later when we lived in upstate New York, I had another chance to take Laura with me. This time I did not forget her. It was quite a drive from East Pembroke to White Plains, New York, where I had an appointment with Birdseye in the General Foods headquarters. This was a large account that registered several hundred thousand dollars for our company. Prior to my taking over the New York territory, the president and senior vice-president of Asgrow would each make the trip from New Haven, Connecticut. I assured them both that I was prepared and could handle the account. We arrived, and after the first half hour of the visit, Laura was fidgeting and said that she had to go potty. Mr. Enzie, the buyer buzzed for his secretary to accompany Laura to the bathroom. We were in the middle of a conversation when Laura came back and said, "Daddy, you should see their pretty potty. It is beautiful; they have real flowers in there, and it is so clean. The nice lady let me go all by myself, and I even flushed like you tell me to at home". I was 'flushing' too as Laura went on about how the floors were very shiny, the soap smelled like flowers, and the towels were real and soft and fluffy. Mr. Enzie, a grandfather, was getting a big chuckle out of her. I told her, "Okay, honey, but daddy has more work to do". The rest of the meeting went well and Laura sat there like a little angel. As we were getting ready to leave, Mr. Enzie smiled at Laura and told her she was welcome to come back any time, adding, "Oh, by the way, I know where there is a lollipop for you".

Never underestimate the power or innocence of a child– anonymous

Next, it was Jennifer's turn to go. Jennifer was just 14 months younger than Laura, and I knew she would like the Beech Nut factory in Canajoharie, New York. The name of the city, by the way, is a Mohawk Indian word meaning "the pot that washes itself". My visit to the factory included traveling the fields with Chuck Jones who was in charge of the agricultural division. At this huge plant, they packed all kinds of baby food and used train-car loads of our seed for their vegetable plantings. Fortunately, they were harvesting, and Jennifer was wide-eyed at the huge combines. Later, Chuck gave us a tour of the factory where jars of baby food were flying by at speeds of 100 or more per minute. The other and better part of the plant was even more appealing. This was where Life Savers and gum of all flavors were packed filling the air with mint and other great aromas. Jennifer, who was never bashful, tugged at Chuck's white coat and said, "Mr. Jones, I am too big for baby food, but I do like candy and gum". She looked at me for approval, but before I could say anything, there was a large bag being filled with all different flavors of gum and candy. The visit and the tour were great, and Jennifer topped it off by saying, "Thank you nice man".

Our son Jeff was probably the youngest to experience a tour with me through the country side while on business. He was strapped securely in his car seat, and I was armed with plenty of small snacks to keep him occupied. I pointed out many of the things we passed like you would on a sight-seeing trip, but boredom set in and his head gradually lowered into his bag of treats. My list of things to do did not include going into a customer's office, but instead examining the health of crops and small talk with the local growers.

After giving Nancy a three hour break, we headed back home. Jeff's way of saying he appreciated the bonding was the big grin I received as I lifted him out of the car.

YES, THERE IS A KALAMAZOO

In 1968, I was asked to move to the home office in New Haven, Connecticut. It seemed like in a short time, a pharmaceutical company from Kalamazoo, Michigan sent their top officers to tour our facility. Our home office was a masterpiece that graced architectural magazines showing our site on 30 acres overlooking the Merritt Parkway. We had a stocked pond, and just like the Peabody Hotel in Memphis, at a certain hour, the ducks would parade through the building, greet a few people, and leave. The woods contained a variety of different trees, and at the entrance to the office building there was a winding road bedecked with flowers that bloomed in the different seasons. The offices were spacious with individual office doors made of walnut that went from the floor to the ceiling.

There was some chatter about Upjohn buying our company, and this was confirmed a few years later. Upjohn was the first of a string of pharmaceutical companies to buy a seed company. There was a nice fit with their veterinarian division and food (seed) which in many countries superseded vaccines.

As with many global companies, the headquarters had its own teaching center and select employees were exposed to various courses. One class that I took was a speech class where we were asked to deliver with vigor a pet peeve. We were told to put lots of meaning into our statements, and even pound on the table if we wanted. My pet peeve was having bread in a basket at a restaurant where most of the bread was not cut all the way through so when you picked up a slice, you got the whole loaf.

There were some great deliveries on peeves about people showing up late, slow lines at sporting events, and an older married guy complaining that his mother-in-law was always stopping by. Two that I remember so vividly were: Toshio Menaka saying he had a bottom floor apartment and there was a lot of "noisy". If he had said it once, it would not have been as funny, but he repeated, "Loud 'noisy' coming down from the radiator", or as he said, 'ladiatol'. When he would try to concentrate, more "noisy". "Noisy" when I am trying to study is a pet peeve. The other one is a classic! Bill was a lanky basketball player from one of the Big Ten schools who either started or was the back- up center. He went to the podium, had a scowl on his face, pounded the wood, and shouts out, "Pet peeves piss me off.....they really do". Just as with Toshio, I was laughing until my sides hurt. To top it off, he goes one more time at it, and as he is walking towards the audience, he blurts out, "I can't tell you enough times how pet peeves really do piss me off".

A Fun Day at the Bay of Fundy

The Bay of Fundy separates Maine from both New Brunswick and Nova Scotia. The world's largest bathtub sits in St. John, New Brunswick; the town where I was staying. The tides in that bay are the world's largest at 55 feet. The bay itself is 100 miles long , 62 miles wide, and 400 to 700 feet deep.

The three Maritime providences of New Brunswick, Nova Scotia, and Prince Edward Island were part of the territory I inherited after a colleague retired. It was a cold Sunday with a gray-blue sky. I had attended 7:30am Mass, going to a local diner for a hearty breakfast afterwards. The hail had just stopped so I mentioned to the waitress that Mary must have taken me literally when I said the "Hail Mary". She got a kick out of that. I knew of the tides, but did not check on the times they come in and out. Now I know it is every six hours although on that particular day I had not learned this yet. I decided to kill some time by taking a drive noticing several paths where vehicles had driven off the road to the beach. I selected one such path. It was clear and obviously used quite a bit. I drove down to the beach, parked the car, saw a lot of driftwood, and decided to go for a walk. I started picking up nice unique pieces of the wood putting them in piles. For the next two to three hours I walked for a couple of miles figuring I would rest a bit, get a quick soft drink, then walk back to select the best driftwood from the piles to put in the trunk of the car. I thought to myself maybe I could even get a cardboard box and ship my treasures home. After my break, I started to head back and noticed some of the piles that were on land were now completely submerged. Continuing to walk back my eyes couldn't believe what I saw when I finally rounded the bend. My car was a good hundred feet out in the bay with water up to the door handles! After running back to the restaurant to ask if there was a garage open on Sunday, I was assured there was. The wonderful woman called the BP station to relate my story. A man on duty said he would pick me up in a vehicle that had a wench large enough to pull the car out, and that it did!!! After getting me on dry land I asked if he would tow me to the airport so I could turn the car in to get another one. The first thing the driver asked me was what prompted me to turn off the highway. I said that I had seen very many tire tracks through the grass and sand leading to the beach. He then told me those tracks were made by people with boats and other water craft.

Our company policy was not to purchase insurance on rental cars as the cost on the many rentals did not justify the few claims they had each year. On this trip a sweet, young clerk had asked me about insurance, and I told her of our policy. She said she would recommend it because so many tourists gawked at the sights and that accidents were quite common. I sensed she made some money writing the policy and felt sorry for her. Thinking maybe she was working hard to save money for college, I said okay, but I would need a separate receipt so that I could pay for it out of my own pocket. Later as I was driving around I got to thinking, what gawkers? This was early October, and the tourist season was usually June through September. No wonder the beach was empty except me, and thank God it wasn't during prime season. Can you even imagine the pile up as tourists strained their necks to see some foreigner with his car being buried by the incoming tide? When the tow truck unloaded me at the airport, I was soaking wet, but the car was even worse. The car rental agent was amazed that I got the car out in time telling me how fortunate I was to have taken out insurance. Maybe, just maybe, it was the "Hail Mary" or the "Lord's Prayer" I said in church that saved me. I am thinking in this case it was both.

THE REAL MCCOY

Somehow I got dirt in my left eye so that it was swollen and badly infected. The doctor gave me some eye drops to apply in the morning and before bed, told me to wear a black patch, and get plenty of rest. When I told him I had to attend a convention in Chicago, the National Food Processor's Convention, he said no. When I insisted that I had to attend he agreed to let me go as long as I got plenty of rest. I promised to be in bed every night at 8 pm, no later.

Our salespeople had invited a small group for dinner at the Knickerbocker Hotel, not too far from the Drake where we were staying. Everyone was going into town after dinner, but I declined since I had promised my doctor an early evening. I remembered I had to lie down to place the drops he prescribed exactly into the eye and then close my eyes for 15 minutes. As soon as I got to my room the phone rang. It was Dr. Liddell, our advertising man, who said he said he felt sorry for me and would get some coffee, bring it up to my room, and visit for a while as I was relaxing on the bed. Not wanting to get up, I told him I would leave the door ajar because I would have the towel over my eyes. When the door opened I did not look up thinking it was Dr. Liddell. It turned out to be a lady of the evening who must have been walking the halls looking for action. She may have figured that I had passed out. Thinking it was Dr. Liddell, I said, "Thanks for coming in; I really appreciate the company". When I took the towel off my eyes, the person who introduced herself as Felicia asked if I wanted her company. I said, "Oh no, I am waiting for my good friend, Bill, who should be here any minute". She fired back, "I hope you have an enjoyable fling you queer pervert"!

OPTIONS AND A COVETED AWARD

With about six to seven years left in my career, I was contacted by a large Fortune 500 company regarding the taking of a position as Vice President of Agriculture. I listened carefully, jotted down notes and questions, and said that I would think about it. I had two more calls, and was impressed with the company and the initial salary offer that was climbing, now into six figures. Our family had moved three times and with such a few years left in the peak of my career, I respectfully declined. I was aware of the friends our children had made, and it would be tough on them to move again. Next, I was asked if I knew any other potential candidates, to think about it, and to call back in a couple days. I called a person who was heavily involved with the daily scheduling of crops and who had 15 or so years experience with a much smaller, but national firm. He said that he would consider the position, and called me back in a couple weeks saying that he went for the interview, was accepted, and he took the job. He sent me a very nice thank you card. Written on the bottom was "See you in New Orleans at the convention". I called him and set a date and time for just the two of us for a quiet, relaxing dinner. When we met, I started by congratulating him and asking trivial questions about his health, how he liked his new job, and how his family was adjusting to the move. After exchanging pleasantries, I got down to talking business. It is strange, but I had not planned my breakthrough discussion ahead of time, but just then when we were sitting across from each other having dinner. I started out by saying, "You have heard the new broom sweeps clean. Well, I would like you to consider a plan that I firmly believe would be a win/win. Here is the plan: the company you are now working for has some duplication with our company. We both have research farms, technicians, breeders, trial plots, and seed production. By allowing us to meld the portion of your agricultural division into ours, you can free up people, land, production facilities, and eliminate inventory". He was taking notes and seemed very enthusiastic about my proposal. I went on to say, "We would hire your breeder and be responsible for storing the surplus seed you now have. Of course, we would like a long term commitment with you, and anyone else in the agriculture department is free to inspect our facilities and tour the seed crop fields". All the other details about confidentiality of hybrids, volumes, acreage, and price would be agreed upon.

It took months of negotiations and meetings, but eventually my plan was coming to fruition. The net result was over a million dollars in added revenue and a lower cost for our product with the increased volume.

I am sure this venture weighed heavily with the upper management when it came time to present the annual Upjohn award. The coveted award is given in October of each year. Twenty recipients are selected from the 20,000 employees so my chances were one in a thousand to have this honor. I was told five years in a row by my boss that I was being considered, later to be told I was nominated, but didn't make it. I kept thinking maybe next year would be my turn.

In 1991, I received a call at home stating that I made the list unanimously and congratulations were in order. After hanging up the phone and telling my wife, I went into the bathroom and cried because it took all my years of hard, dedicated work to achieve an award given to a select few. Besides the hefty cash award, I received increases in salary and stock options. To cap it off, a Christmas gift was sent each year. At the ceremony, it was stated that those being honored exhibited special accomplishments and achievements for the company. It was one of my proudest moments. I aimed high and hit the target!

Don't be afraid of showing your feelings, be afraid of regretting it when you don't – Laura Springer

New Management

A large conglomerate from Mexico purchased our company and wanted top management to move to California to meld in with another company they had purchased. I was just two years away from retirement, and after doing research on retirement places Nancy and I had decided on the St. George, Utah, area. Each director had a chance to meet one on one with the new president to introduce himself and relate his responsibilities. After a minute of cordial greetings, I came right out and said I would like to appoint the product manager who reported to me as my boss. This way I could move to Southern Utah and work and train the new salesperson in the Northwest. After two years I would retire, and before I could say any more, I was given a firm handshake and told I could work as long as I wanted to because it was a very commendable gesture. This was a win/win situation, and after the two years were up, I had compiled 39 years of service and was now ready to settle on a golf course in the quiet, beautiful suburb of St. George.

Retirement

RETIREMENT

When a man retires and time is no longer a matter of urgent importance, he is presented with a watch – R.C. Sheriff

The town, only twenty miles from Zion National Park, is Hurricane, which is located within 120 mile radius of more National Parks and reservoirs than anywhere else in the world. The first year or so was spent furnishing our new home that we built, getting acquainted with friends and neighbors, and playing golf. One day I got a call from a national firm in Canada asking about my desire to consult for them for a couple years. My first impression was no way, but I listened to the offer. When I was asked to name my price, I popped up with twenty hours a month at $350 per hour, a company car, and all expenses. I really didn't care if they accepted the proposal or not, but when they did not hesitate, I figured they wanted my services. As for the car, I said I wanted a Lexus 400 that I could keep after my two year contract was up. After two years passed it was time to finally retire to be fair to my wife who found it difficult to commit to social functions not knowing what my schedule would be.

Later in the year, we drove to Camarillo, California to play golf with some of my business colleagues and have a belated retirement party. My boss was relating the years I spent with the company saying he was amazed how I could pull out of the air an extra 1, 2, 3, or 4 million dollars, if a division needed it to make budget. I would always say, "Consider it done, but I need time to make some phone calls". I pushed hard for these extra sales, offered discounts on the order above what was already sold, guaranteed the price, offered free storage, and delayed payment. It surely helped knowing these multi-generational customers almost 40 years.

Now my goal was to stay home except for a trip to Hawaii and New Zealand which we had been planning for years with the Frohardt's. During my 39 years of service, I had travelled to 43 countries in my job as world-wide sales director. During the first 18 years of my life I ventured no more than 20 miles from where I lived.

What does one do in retirement? Well, anything he or she wants! There is plenty to do besides golf, garden, hike, fish, and read. A real world exists out there where there are the less fortunate who need a hand or an ear for listening and a heart for compassion. At first I joined the local Rotary Club, and then started doing community service like cleaning the roadside of paper and debris, and sponsoring an antique car show for a designated charity or cause.

One day I read an article in the paper saying the Dixie Care and Share needed volunteers to separate, bag, and distribute food donated by local stores for the needy. I jumped at the chance, and handed out food for three hours a day twice a week. Countless needy people came through the doors of the food pantry, and after selecting their needs they would say, "God bless you for taking care of us" or "let me shake your hand". After doing this for 1 ½ years, I was asked by director Ralph Flanagan to be on the board where he felt I could contribute even more like planning for more homes, discussion of grants, and raising funds. They were expanding rapidly and the thousands of pounds of food donated had grown as did the city, the homeless, and the less fortunate.

I suggested having an auction which I would spearhead, mentioning that it could be held at our country club where we had plenty of room and would not need to cart chairs and tables. Director Flanagan said this would be my project, and appointed me head of fund raising. I started calling and asking our country club members to donate something of value from their homes. I guessed right when I figured I had an audience that came to St. George to retire and had old paintings, cases of wine, and the offer of other services such as boat rides, glider trips, fishing trips, and the use of a lodge. Other items were a hand-crafted wind spinner, old guns, silverware, crochet or knit items, and wood working added more to this first auction. My wife lent a helpful hand in typing out descriptions for both the silent and live auction items. Bloomington Country Club members poured out their hearts, cleaned out their attics or garages, and opened their wallets and purses. My friend, Jim Grimm, helped me auction off the items, and 120 people bid to raise almost $18,000. I felt really good, and Director Flanagan came up to me afterwards, gave me a hug, and looked up for a second and said, "Thank you God for sending Lynn to our charity".

We paused a year to give the country club members and ourselves time for a breather and plan the second auction. It was a little easier than the first, and even before I could say something about this next auction I was getting calls saying, "count me in the next time you decide to have another fund raiser" and "I would be more than happy to contribute and help this most worthy cause". As with the first auction, 95% of the items donated were from the Bloomington Country Club members. 116 of the 122 in the bidding audience were members as well. With all of the volunteers that evening things went quite smoothly, but it was still work and many miles put on my car to collect and deliver the donated items. Identical to the first auction, we raised $18,000. It was hard work, but the effort was worth it.

You cannot do charity or kindness too soon, for you never know how soon it will be too late – Ralph Waldo Emerson

A Proud, Poor Church Mouse

Telling my story of growing up to many friends, neighbors, and work associates, they would say, "No doubt, you were as poor as a church mouse". This saying comes about since parishioners rarely brought food to a church service, and if you were a mouse who strayed in from a field or the street, your chances of getting food was pretty slim.

There is, however, a brighter side to this story; even a poor church mouse can contribute something. It was a hungry church mouse that gnawed a hole in the bellows of the old church organ in Oberndorf, Austria. In just a few hours, Josef Mohr and his good friend, Franz Guber perceived that their co-production would someday make them famous. Their main concern was that the traditional Christmas Eve midnight mass might not be entirely devoid of music. With no church organ, the guitar was used, but was seen as a worldly instrument in those days, and was not fit for use in a church. As organist, Guber was probably not very excited about composing a piece for Mohr's guitar. The men were more concerned about how the people would receive the implementation of this instrument than how they would like the new song. The well-known Christmas carol, Silent Night, has not lost any of its allure for millions of people around the globe since it was first played and sung in 1818.

Poor is the church without music– Irish saying

Just recently Nancy and I organized a dinner and a silent auction at the country club for the DOVE House and raised several thousand dollars. This organization provides prevention and treatment to eliminate abuse between partners and stop violence against women and their dependent children.

It was just a couple of weeks after agreeing to be on the board of the DOVE House that I got a call requesting I consider taking the position of fund raiser and be on the board for New Frontiers for Families. This organization is a Utah non-profit organization that provides education advocacy and training as well as direct support to consumers and families with complex needs, to promote self sufficiency, and improve their quality of life. How could one say no to the polite group of youngsters (16 boys) that met me at their house, gave me a tour, and outlined the daily chores expected of them? After cooking hamburgers and hot dogs and mingling with the boys, a few girls and two or three little ones, it was time to eat and give them a short presentation of passages from this book. They could relate to my story since their backgrounds were similar since most were "Lost Boys and Girls" left to fend on their own with some found sleeping behind buildings or in vehicles. They were kicked out of homes, most times for no reason, perhaps because they were an innocent burden. I thought it would make a more lasting impression if I had something to give each person so I put together a packet containing most of the quotations I used in my book. When I finished, I handed each one in the room the quotations and asked that they look at one each day and carry it with them in their wallet or purse. Single sheet copies of all were made for reference that could be displayed in the house. I would like to share with you the list I presented that evening.

1.   *"Reach for the stars and do not be surprised if you catch one" – anonymous*

2.   *"The ultimate measure of a man is not where he stands in moments of comfort and convenience , but where he stands at times of challenge and controversy "– Martin Luther King*

3.   *"Smooth seas do not make skillful sailors" – African proverb*

4.   *"Intense difficulties, hardship, and major obstacles are actually major contributions to success" – Eleanor Roosevelt*

5. *"You can tell how big a person is by what it takes to discourage him" – anonymous*

6. *"Never think you are not good enough for anyone; always ask yourself if they are good enough for you" – anonymous*

7. *"Try less to be accepted, but accept yourself first" – anonymous*

8. *"He who angers you, conquers you" – Elizabeth Kenny*

9. *"The greatest danger for most of us is not that we aim too high and miss, but we aim too low and make it" – Michelangelo*

10. *"Don't be afraid of showing your feelings, be afraid of regretting it when you don't" – Laura Springer*

11. *"Everyone has a burden; what counts is how you carry it" – Merle Miller*

12. *"Those who say they never get a chance, never took one" – anonymous*

13. *"Accept any challenge so you can feel the exhilaration of victory" – General George Patton, Jr.*

14. *"Those who fear the thorns, will never pick the roses" – anonymous*

15. *"When you smile when no one else is around you, you really mean it" – from the Reader's Digest*

16. *"The best way to cheer yourself up; cheer everybody up" – Mark Twain*

17. *"Obstacles and hardships do not have to lead to failure! Adversity causes some men to break and others to break records" – William Ward*

18. *"No one outside of ourselves can rule us inwardly. When we know this we become free" – Buddha*

Since my first encounter with these special kids, I have given several gift certificates for various eating establishments in town. When I asked them what they usually had for dinner, they said in almost unison, "Pizza, because it doesn't cost much".

In my assignment on the board, a fund raising goal of $10,000 has been set for a dinner and silent auction this spring. We are well on our way to achieving that mark with pledges and tables of 6 or 8 purchased already.

Besides the already mentioned charities, we support others – the Saint George Catholic church, Salvation Army, Boy Scouts, cancer research, and the March of Dimes. Monthly contributions are given to the Covenant House serving the homeless and runaway children at risk. World Vision is another of our favorites. It is a Christian relief and development organization whose goal is working for the well being of all people, especially children. Each year at Christmas we would buy chickens or goats for the poor in Jamaica; that was our gift to each other. This year we decided to buy a house for their shelter and protection. During our first twenty years of marriage, we gave what we could to the church, but funding three children in college all at the same time was difficult. After seeing all three graduate and being at the peak of my earning years, we began giving more and more. Over the past twenty years our donations in prayer, time, and most of all money, would exceed hundreds of thousands of dollars.

I will always remember, What you keep to yourself, you lose. What you give away, you keep forever - anonymous